Casa Florida

Casa Florida

SPANISH-STYLE HOUSES FROM WINTER PARK TO CORAL GABLES

Susan Sully

PHOTOGRAPHY BY **Steven Brooke**

RIZZOLI
NEW YORK

First published in the United States of America in 2005
by Rizzoli International Publications, Inc.
300 Park Avenue South, New York, NY 10010
www.rizzoliusa.com

ISBN: 0-8478-2703-8
Library of Congress Control Number: 2005902662

Copyright © 2005 Rizzoli International Publications, Inc.
Text copyright © 2005 Susan Sully
Photographs copyright © 2005 Steven Brooke
Designed by Element group

Printed in China

Endpapers: Spanish tiles imported by Walter DeGarmo to decorate the 1921 Coconut Grove house he designed for his family.

Frontis: The white-painted filigree of Mrs. William Orr's interior gate offsets the severity of the exterior entrance hall, easing the transition from the austere facade to the welcoming courtyard space.

Opposite: The interior of the antique Spanish door of the Cielito Lindo house at 123 Kings Road is carved with eight-pointed Islamic stars, indicating the Moorish influence upon Andalusian Spanish style.

Page 6: With white stucco walls, red clay tiles, and varying roof heights, this house typifies the austere yet sensual Spanish style Florida-based architects created for wealthy clients during the boom years.

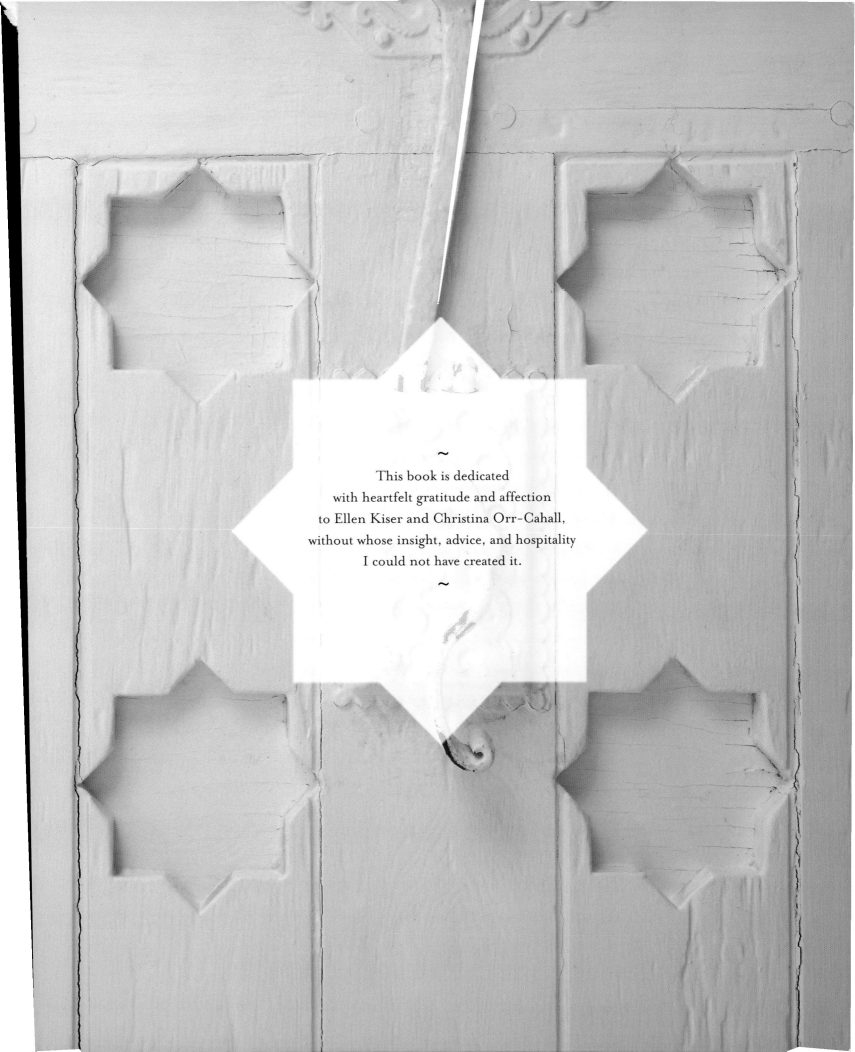

~

This book is dedicated
with heartfelt gratitude and affection
to Ellen Kiser and Christina Orr-Cahall,
without whose insight, advice, and hospitality
I could not have created it.

~

THE FLORIDA JUNGLE IS AN AMAZINGLY FASCINATING PLACE . . .
*and yet in 1927 . . . a certain part of this jungle had completely
vanished, and in its place had arisen a stately residence,
with walls of old-ivory and roofs of rose, set in vast gardens
of blue, emerald and mauve, the colors of the tropical sea
twilight; and within, a home so gracious and lovely, so
complete in every final detail that the story of the jungle
seems an improbable fairy-tale.*

—MARY FANTON ROBERTS, from a description of Cielito Lindo in Palm Beach
published in *Arts & Decoration*, July 1928

BUT LOOK OUT FROM MIZNER'S WINDOW AND SEE THE TRUE
*Florida skyline—those red tiled roofs, peaked, variable, at
different elevations, and all at such a height that the thing
which makes the most beauty against the sky in all Florida, the
palm, receives its full value.*

—IDA M. TARBELL, from "The Appreciation of a Layman," published in the 1928
first edition of *Florida Architecture of Addison Mizner*

CONTENTS

10   INTRODUCTION
Five Centuries of Spanish Style:
An Enduring Legacy

42   Buenos Recuerdos
A 1927 Spanish-Style Villa in Palm Beach

52   The DeGarmo Estate
A 1921 Courtyard Villa in Coconut Grove, Miami

62   Casita Collage
A Circa-1920 West Palm Beach Casita

72   House of Tiles
A 1922 Spanish-Style Villa in Palm Beach

82   Villa Mizner
A 1924 Tower Residence on Via Mizner in Palm Beach

92   Eclectic Elegance
A Mid-1920s Spanish-Style House on Snell Isle, St. Petersburg

100   Casa Mia
A 1925 Ferro-Concrete Spanish Villa in Coral Gables

108   The Don Quixote House
A 1926 Coral Gables Casita

116   Cielito Lindo
A 1928 Mediterranean Revival Mansion in Palm Beach

126   Nuestro Paradiso
A 1928 Palm Beach Mansion

136   Timeless Style
A 1932 Spanish-Style House in St. Petersburg

144   Spanish Modern
A 1934 Art Deco/Spanish-Style House in Miami Beach

154   House of Stone
A 1936 Coral Rock Cottage in Coral Gables

166   El Cortijo
A 1937 Country Spanish-Style House in Winter Park

174   Ranch Redux
A Remodeled Ranch House in Miami

182   Hispano-Modern
A 2000 Modernist Mediterranean Revival House in Coconut Grove

192   Palazzo delle Aquile
*An Early-Twenty-First-Century Mediterranean Revival Mansion
in Winter Park*

205   Acknowledgments

208   Index

Antique Spanish tile paves the entrance court of a Palm Beach villa designed by Marion Sims Wyeth in 1922. Tile appears throughout the house, accenting an exterior staircase and balcony above the entrance court, lining courtyards, and decorating walls.

INTRODUCTION

Five Centuries of Spanish Style:

AN ENDURING LEGACY

When Ponce de Leon and his Spanish crew first viewed the northern shores of Florida in March 1513, "believing that this land was an island, they named it *La Florida*, because it has a very beautiful view of many cool woodlands, . . . and because, moreover, they discovered it in the time of the Feast of Flowers." So wrote Antonio de Herrera, royal historiographer of Spain, explaining that the explorer was following a tip from the indigenous people of Puerto Rico, who had described for him a land rich in gold and graced with a magic fountain restoring youth.[1] This name and the fantasy of riches and restored youthfulness are two of the three lasting legacies the Spanish gave to the state of Florida. The third is the romantic notion of Spanish architecture—based more upon a latter-day American desire to create a regional style of building appropriate to Florida than upon actual architectural remains of the Spanish settlement.

"Although the presence of the Spanish in Florida's past could provide a memory upon which to draw inspiration," writes Jose Lozano in an article about Walter DeGarmo and Richard Kiehnel (two progenitors of the state's Spanish and Mediterranean revival styles), "no significant, tangible legacy remained in the form of architecture. . . . The massive fort of San Marco in St. Augustine, the only structure of any significance built by the Spanish in Florida, could provide early south Florida architects with a suitable typology only if future towns were to appear as gigantic military fortifications."[2]

Fifty years after Ponce de Leon claimed Florida for the Spanish crown, St. Augustine was established as a Spanish military base—a precarious outpost frequently attacked during the two centuries between its establishment in 1565 and its transfer to British authority in 1763. "Drake of England burned the settlement in 1586, freebooters sacked it in 1668,

Opposite: At Henry Flagler's request, architects Carrère and Hastings created a Spanish-style design for the Ponce de Leon Hotel in St. Augustine. The design marries elements of Spanish and Italian Renaissance palaces and cloisters, presaging Florida's early-twentieth-century Mediterranean revival style.

South Carolinians besieged and burned it in 1702, and British troops bombarded it in 1740," writes Albert Manucy in his study of the city's early domestic architecture, *The Houses of St. Augustine*.[3]

Despite the destructive effect of these events upon the settlement, as well as the inevitable decay brought about by the humid climate, a cohesive architectural type revealing the influence of Spain survived into the late eighteenth century. A Quaker botanist named John Bartram, who visited following Britain's 1763 acquisition of the colony, described several residences sharing many elements in common with the Spanish-style houses built by American architects 150 years later.[4] His account describes cantilevered covered balconies, arcaded loggias, flat-roofed houses constructed of "hewn shell stone" called coquina, tabby (an early form of concrete), or wood. These were equipped with stone battlements and "pipes, mostly of burnt clay, let through the wall and projecting a foot or more to carry off the water." The houses had plentiful, large windows, some of which had "a lattice with holes one inch square"—a detail that seems to have been the precursor of the decorative screens of wood or wrought iron employed by late-nineteenth- and early-twentieth-century architects.

While Manucy states that no house remaining in St. Augustine predates 1703, he asserts that approximately thirty dwellings from the 1700s, mostly stone, survived

The central courtyard of the Ponce de Leon (now Flagler College) features a shaded arcade with Roman arches, a campanile, cantilevered balconies, and red clay tiles, all elements that were to become central to the vocabulary of Florida's Spanish style.

into the twentieth century. The Saint Augustine Historical Society maintains what is considered to be Florida's oldest surviving Spanish Colonial dwelling, the González-Alvarez House, as a museum called the Oldest House. These structures formed part of the inspiration for the first of Florida's Spanish-style resorts: Henry Flagler's Ponce de Leon Hotel, completed in St. Augustine in 1889 and designed by the New York–based architects John Carrère and Thomas Hastings, who were employed by the famed architectural firm of McKim, Mead, and White before forming their own firm, Carrère & Hastings. "I wanted to retain the Spanish character of St. Augustine, and so designed the buildings in keeping with the architecture of the early houses here with their quaint overhanging balconies," Hastings explained after designing the hotel.[5]

This reliance upon the historic Spanish-informed vernacular architecture of Florida was an extreme rarity among the late-nineteenth- and early-twentieth-century architects who forged the state's Spanish and Mediterranean revival styles. Equally unusual was the fact that the two architects, at the behest of their wealthy patron Flagler, spent two years

studying the architecture of Spain firsthand, making sketches and collecting ideas, before designing the hotel. The result was a huge and lavish fantasy occupying an entire city block. Composed of coquina and cement, the imposing structure combines early Spanish Renaissance motifs and details with a touch of the Italian Renaissance, including a grand gateway loosely modeled upon the gate of the Certosa at Pavia. In this last detail, Carrère and Hastings introduced two elements of the mélange of influences that was to become the extensive and eclectic design vocabulary of Spanish and Mediterranean revival–style architecture in Florida.

Neither of these terms accurately describes the freewheeling, romantic quotation of pan-Mediterranean sources that defined Florida's prevailing architectural style of the late nineteenth and early twentieth centuries. The term *Spanish style* implies a monolithic reliance upon mainland Spanish architecture as source. In certain buildings, Florida's architects did indeed reveal such faithful adoption and adaptation of Iberian design. However, they also drew upon Spanish Colonial forms from Mexico and South

In contrast to the coquina, cement, and terracotta details of the exterior, the Ponce de Leon's gilded and frescoed rotunda seems to borrow more from Italian Renaissance design than Spanish sources.

American countries. These same architects might also combine Florentine, Roman, Venetian, and/or North African details, thus veering into the realm of what became known as the Mediterranean revival, a term that also has limitations in that it suggests the existence of a unified Mediterranean architecture revived by these modern architects.

While there is clear evidence of the sharing of certain architectural forms and ornamentation among the civilizations that traveled the Mediterranean Sea, each country and each age had its own distinct architecture. The process of borrowing and combining so many of these into a collective architectural style was an American invention born of late Victorian eclecticism that matured in Florida's early-twentieth-century romantic resort design. "Spanish, Italian, Moorish, Byzantine . . . are under this orchestrated process merged . . . into a sun-loving style," explained Rexford Newcomb in his 1928 study entitled *Mediterranean Domestic Architecture in the United States.*[6] For descriptive purposes in this book, the term *Spanish style* is used to describe buildings of nearly pure Spanish influence, and the term *Mediterranean revival* is employed to describe those that reveal a more eclectic mix of styles.

It is indisputable that these styles, no matter how named, are a distinctly Floridian legacy, developed by a handful of imaginative, well-trained architects financed by the visionary transportation, hospitality, and real estate magnates who recognized in Florida fertile ground for growing escapist fantasies. Flagler, the Standard Oil tycoon and mastermind of the Florida East Coast Railway and luxury hotels linked by it, is often attributed with bringing the Spanish revival style to Florida. However, the style had already found expression in St. Augustine in the form of *Villa Zorayda*, the winter home of Boston hardware merchant Franklin W. Smith—a self-trained architect who had designed miniature replicas of great buildings from around the world since childhood.

For his larger-than-life St. Augustine home, named for a character in Washington Irving's *Tales of the Alhambra*,[7] Smith took inspiration from southern Spain's Alhambra palace. Made of coquina and concrete, and completed in 1885, the house presented faithful reproductions of architectural elements from Andalusia, as southern Spain became known during its period of Moorish occupation. Beehive-shaped cornice details; decorative screens of polychromed, turned wood; horseshoe arches; and colorful, patterned tile were among the Moorish details Smith incorporated in his design. The interior was decorated with "inlaid and elaborately carved Oriental pieces, ancient Egyptian hangings, valuable rugs, ancient firearms, and many Oriental items," according to the 1939 WPA guide to Florida.

This inventory marks Smith's design impulse as one rooted within late-nineteenth-century, Victorian Orientalism—a short-lived design craze that popularized Moorish ornamentation on both sides of the Atlantic. While Flagler was reportedly quite impressed with *Villa Zorayda*, and may have been influenced by its coquina and cement construction, he and his architects diverged from the Andalusian influence of Orientalism, opting instead for the grand style of Renaissance-era Spain—a conscious reference to the origins of Florida's founder, the hotel's namesake, Ponce de Leon. With its long masonry wings

Opposite: Vine-covered loggias create a transition between the sun-drenched cloister and the cool, well-shaded interior spaces of the Boca Raton Resort & Club.

Above: Two-story barrel-vaulted ceilings with clerestory windows provide for the maximum natural flow of air and light in Mizner's 1925 hotel, revealing his genius not only for creating dramatic public spaces but also functional ones.

stretching along two sides of a courtyard accented by a splashing fountain, its arcades, loggias, cantilevered balconies, slender towers, and red barrel tile roof, the building presaged the style that was to gain sway throughout the state in the coming three decades.

Constructed over a period of a year and a half, the 540-room hotel opened to ecstatic praise in 1889. According to Flagler's biographer, Les Standiford, "the national press proclaimed it superior to hotels such as Chicago's Palmer House and San Francisco's Palace, and socialites flocked southward to experience this Babylon, where even the meanest room featured electric lights and had cost one thousand dollars to decorate."[8] The success of the Ponce de Leon Hotel encouraged Flagler to construct a sister property in St. Augustine named the Alcazar. Inspired by the royal palace in Seville, this hotel featured towers, arcades, loggias, and red roof tiles as well.

Having transformed St. Augustine from a sleepy resort for a handful of wintering northeasterners and midwesterners to a thriving tourist town with a distinctly Spanish

Previous: Mizner's Ritz-Carlton Cloister, now the Boca Raton Resort & Club, features a magnificently landscaped cloister flanked by two wings featuring inviting loggias, varied fenestration, and a crown of fanciful Gothic pinnacles.

flavor, Flagler turned his attention to the problem of getting his guests there. When his hotels first opened, the trip to St. Augustine entailed a train ride to Jacksonville, a cruise down the St. Johns River, and a short ride down a narrow-gauge railroad track.[9] Flagler purchased the Jacksonville, St. Augustine & Halifax River Line and built a bridge over the St. Johns River, thus extending full rail service to his hotel properties. This launched Flagler's dual investment in rail service and luxury hotels that ultimately linked St. Augustine, Ormand Beach, Miami, Palm Beach, and Key West, among other lesser-known destinations.

During the last decade of the nineteenth century, Flagler found a competitor in Henry Plant, an entrepreneur who purchased narrow-gauge railroads in southern Florida with the goal of linking Tampa to Miami. Plant, who established Tampa as a major Gulf of Mexico port by building a deep-water pier, constructed his own grand hotel, the Tampa Bay Hotel, which opened in 1891. Unlike Flagler, whose architects presaged the full-blown Spanish and Mediterranean revival styles of the early twentieth century in their choice of materials and design sources, Plant and his architect, New York–based J. A. Wood, remained firmly rooted within Victorian building methods and period exoticism, creating a massive red brick structure decorated in unrestrained Moorish Orientalism.

Described by historian William Seale as "one of the most fanciful creations of America's Gilded Age," the hotel's facade features long wood porches decorated with Moorish arches outlined with intricate wood filigree. An eclectic array of French, Italian, Asian, and Spanish furnishings and artwork decorated the hotel's 402 guest rooms, dining rooms, music rooms, and ballrooms. Twelve towers top the fantastical building, crowned with silver onion domes sporting silver crescents that pierce the mercurial coastal sky. The WPA guide describes the hotel's opening as a "social sensation . . . attended by 2,000, among them princes, dukes and duchesses, and celebrities of the financial, theatrical, and literary world."[10] However, nationwide financial and political woes dogged the hotel during its forty years of operation, and during the Spanish-American War it was transformed into headquarters for American officers. By the 1930s, the building's present-day occupant, the University of Tampa, had moved in. This institution has maintained the structure in excellent condition and operates a museum on the premises celebrating its colorful past.

Although the Ponce de Leon remained in operation as a hotel until 1967, its popularity also waned in the late nineteenth century in response to outside forces—the most dramatic being the freezes of 1894 and 1895. By that time, Flagler had already extended his empire to Palm Beach, with a railroad line reaching West Palm Beach and a new hotel named the Royal Ponciana opening in 1894. Within another two years, Flagler had opened the Palm Beach Inn, which later became the Breakers. Neither of these sprawling wood hotels, both designed by architects McDonald and McGuire, followed in the stylistic footsteps of the Ponce de Leon. The Breakers's present-day Italianate Renaissance–style appearance dates from a 1925 reconstruction following a fire that destroyed the all-wood building.

The Spanish and Mediterranean revival–style architecture that was to gain widespread popularity among Palm Beach's elite visitors and homeowners did not appear on the island until 1919, when Addison Mizner and Paris Singer built the Everglades Club. When Mizner arrived in Palm Beach in 1918, at the behest of his friend Singer, heir to the sewing machine company's fortune, the island's architecture had thus far evolved as a reflection of turn-of-the-nineteenth-century Northeastern styles. Mizner, who had made an informal study of Spanish Colonial architecture in Guatemala and of Spanish mainland styles in Spain, and had apprenticed in California under Willis Polk, a principal proponent of the Spanish Mission style, brought a new vision to Palm Beach. Born in California, Mizner found success as an architect for the Northeast's elite members of society, building country homes influenced by Japanese, Norman, and Spanish styles, French chateaux, and English country manors, among others.

Mizner came to Palm Beach as Singer's guest to convalesce from a bout of recurring ill health. Singer, who had established a number of hospitals in Europe, decided to create a convalescent home for shell-shocked World War I soldiers on Palm Beach. According to architectural historian Donald Curl, Singer asked Mizner to describe a suitable architecture for the island, and the architect envisioned "a Moorish tower, like on the south coast of Spain, with an open loggia at one side facing the sea." When Mizner contemplated the site of the convalescent home, he reportedly replied that the spot made him think of something religious, "a nunnery, with a chapel built into the lake . . . a mixture built by a nun from Venice, added onto by one from Verona, with a bit of new Spain of the tropics."[11]

Singer moved forward with his planned convalescent home, and Mizner (according to Curl) convinced him to "build a permanent structure for use as a private club after the war."[12] Before the year ended, the armistice was declared, and Singer changed the name of the Touchstone Convalescent Club to the Everglades Club. By January 1919, the exclusive club was complete. "While visitors to St. Augustine . . . might previously have seen Flagler's Ponce de Leon and Alcazar Hotels, nothing could have prepared them for Addison's gorgeous pink stucco palace, with arcades, wrought-iron balconies, and terra-cotta-tile roofs, shimmering like a fairy-tale castle along the shore of Lake Worth," writes Mizner biographer Caroline Seebohm.[13]

Modeled after the Giralda Tower in Seville, the Miami-Biltmore Hotel (1925) is one of the great public places of George Merrick's Coral Gables, which also included a golf course, a country club, and the famed and fanciful Venetian pool.

The clubhouse's Lake Worth facade included the curved cornice and small dome-shaped towers reminiscent of Spanish Colonial religious architecture, while other aspects of the building, including a cloistered garden, central tower, and spiral stair on the Worth Avenue facade reflect mainland Spanish architecture.[14] The interior included Mizner's originally envisioned nun's chapel: a massive dining hall with carved paneling taken from a Spanish church and a soaring, trussed ceiling of pecky cypress. The lobby featured a staircase that spiraled, seemingly unsupported, through the lofty space. The tower included a large apartment for Singer with numerous luxurious amenities, among them a Moorish-style tiled bathroom.

While Mizner reported that the club's style met with criticism during construction from some locals who preferred the conventional wood construction of Flagler's resorts, when the Everglades Club opened in January 1919, it won unstinting praise. A writer from the *Palm Beach Post* complimented Mizner, writing, "Instead of repeating the common and hideous mistake that has been perpetrated all through Florida of using a style of architecture adapted to northern surroundings and a bleak and repellent climate, [Mizner] has searched Italy, Spain and Northern Africa for a model, and has used a blended, softened type of color and line that will prove a revelation."[15]

With the construction of the Everglades Club, Florida's modern Spanish revival style was born. It was immediately embraced by wealthy winter patrons, who commissioned Mizner to build them villas as picturesque and impressive as the Everglades Club. While Mizner began building these residences at a dizzying pace, training workmen and importing building materials,

The loggia paralleling the swimming pool at the Miami-Biltmore Hotel recalls the stately, statuary strewn arcades of Italy's famous Renaissance gardens.

C. Perry Snell planned several public spaces for Snell Isle, the development he created on a mangrove island overlooking St. Petersburg's northeast shore. Amenities included the Sunset Club (1920), whose horseshoe arches, onion domes, and minaret demonstrate the fanciful appeal of Andalusian design.

decorative details, and furnishings from abroad, he also created factories to produce reproductions of ancient stone doorways, carved wood details, and colorful enameled tile to meet the growing demand. Other architects joined the fray, among them Marion Sims Wyeth (designer of the famed Mar-a-Lago), Maurice Fatio, and Julius Jacobs, who all created handsome summer villas on the junglelike shores of Palm Beach.

Describing the natural landscape into which these fantastical villas were scattered, 1920s style writer Mary Fanton Roberts wrote,

The Florida jungle is an amazingly fascinating place, and if one has the courage to penetrate its depth, even a little way in a wheel chair, covered with mosquito netting, and a Negro boy to wheel one out swiftly if the air is too oppressive, there is a sense of almost unearthly beauty that in no way belongs to man, but is perfect in its kind, and is sinister only when man invades it. And so I used to feel a little sad, driving along the Boulevard, with that gorgeous green and violet and rose sea pounding so close on one side, and the great jungle brooding and silent and dangerous on the other.[16]

In the center of this wilderness, Singer and Mizner continued to expand was what to become the civic heart of Palm Beach, creating a golf course, adding on to the Everglades Club, and lining Worth Avenue with architecture reminiscent of the streets of old Spain. Mizner's wish to re-create the intimate, picturesque, Old World charm of that country's ancient cities found expression in Via Mizner and Via Parigi in 1924 and 1925, meandering pedestrian walkways built into a pastel stucco labyrinth of architectural forms. "The combination of public walkway, commercial space, and private residence creates the excitement of the Vias," writes Mizner scholar Christina Orr-Cahall.[17] "At each turn there was a new discovery—a garden spot with a restaurant, an overhanging balcony laden with bougainvillea, a tiled stairway surprisingly tucked beneath a bridge, and always little shops to tantalize."

Mizner was so delighted with the success of this small-scale foray into urban planning that he began to envision the creation of an entire island community of his own design—entirely Spanish in style—on nearby Boca Raton. Mizner formed a development corporation in 1925 and began advertising "the world's most architecturally beautiful playground." He designed and supervised the construction of the Ritz-Carlton Cloister (now the Boca Raton Resort & Club), a hotel with a comparatively severe exterior ornamented with Gothic pinnacles, vine-covered loggias, and a Romanesque arched entrance. The hotel had two long wings extending on either side of a magnificent cloister. The development's property sold well, and Mizner built an administrative building patterned after El Greco's Toledo home. Residences both large and modest were in the planning stages when the Florida land market collapsed in 1926, and the ensuing hurricanes of 1926 and 1928 delivered the final blow to Mizner's grand dream.

Mizner was not alone in pursuing fantastic visions of idealized resort communities along Florida's southern shores. "Following Henry Flagler's railroad, which opened southeast Florida for development, Carl Fisher's Dixie Highway and Henry Ford's flivver made it available to a large American middle class," writes Curl. "Coolidge prosperity gave many the ability to enjoy a holiday in Florida's mild winter climate and to consider owning their own vacation houses. The prosperity convinced others that their fortunes lay in Florida land."[18] These others included Carl G. Fisher, founder of the Indianapolis Speedway and primary developer of Miami Beach, and George E. Merrick, son of a Miami-area pioneer and fruit farmer and founder of Coral Gables.

Fisher helped complete the first bridge from the Florida mainland to Miami Beach, dredged Biscayne Bay to transform mangrove swamps into valuable waterfront property, and constructed the north-south road system that became Dixie Highway.[19] He built the brightly domed Flamingo Hotel on Miami Beach in 1920, created sports attractions, planted a tropical landscape on the sandy soil, and quickly sold commercial and residential property with the flourish of a practiced impresario.

Unlike Fisher, who demonstrated no real concern about architectural unity, Merrick envisioned a stylistically coherent ideal city for Coral Gables, almost three thousand acres on the outskirts of Miami that he began to develop in 1921. Before beginning construction, he created a master plan including residential lots of varying size, wide avenues and narrow streets, picturesque gates leading into different areas, a business district, an inn, a country club, and a golf course, all in keeping with rigorous architectural guidelines to be enforced by the Coral Gables Construction Company. The developer hired a staff of expert engineers, landscape architects, and architects to refine and realize these plans, including Phineas Paist, who served as art director for the community, Kiehnel, DeGarmo, and others.

While Mizner is widely attributed with introducing the mature Spanish style of architecture to Florida in the early twentieth century, Kiehnel (whose firm Kiehnel & Elliott designed the 1918 Coconut Grove residence named El Jardin, now the Carrolton School) and DeGarmo are among the architects most widely associated with developing the Mediterranean revival style. "While the predominant feeling of the architecture of Coral Gables is Spanish, the designers who have worked on the different plazas, gateways, houses and other buildings have wisely refrained from narrowing their conception of the style to anything like an academic formula," wrote Matlack Price in a January 1925 article in *Arts & Decoration* magazine.[20] "Because the buildings of Coral Gables derive from Italy, from the Riviera and from Algiers, as well as from Spain, which is their main source, a collective name, 'Mediterranean,' must be applied. Historically, appropriate for Florida, Spanish architecture has very properly been the fashion there for some time—but Coral Gables promises to develop a style distinctly its own, and to render that style in a highly individualistic technique."

In his extensive article written at the height of Coral Gables's development, Price enumerated many of the details of material, color, and ornamentation that became the accepted vocabulary of the Mediterranean revival style. He describes "stuccoed houses of quaint and unexpected profile . . . tinted in unusual shades of tan, yellow, sienna, and light, dull reds, greys and browns," patios "with an arcade of slender Moorish arches," "natural coral rock, 'antiqued' stucco and old Cuban roof tiles," "arches, loggias and balconies," and "Spanish grille-work of turned and polychromed wood."

Many of the structures Price described remain intact today in Coral Gables, which miraculously maintained its distinctive appearance despite the collapse of Merrick's company in the fall of the Florida land boom. Among the best-known features of the development are the 1925 Miami-Biltmore Hotel, an imposing Spanish-style edifice inspired by the Giralda tower in Seville and designed by Schultz & Weaver, and the Venetian Pool, the picturesque aquatic club furnished with towers, a pergola-covered terrace, and decorated gondola mooring posts.

While Coral Gables and Miami Beach were booming along the southeastern shore of Florida, St. Petersburg was experiencing dramatic expansion as well. After a slow start as a farming community in 1876, St. Petersburg was linked by rail to Sanford, Florida, in 1888 by the Orange Belt Line, a railroad built by Russian exile Piotr Alexeitch Dementieff, who named the town after his birthplace. Its population grew from three hundred at the time of its 1892 incorporation to more than fourteen thousand by 1920,

exploding to fifty thousand by 1925.[21] C. Perry Snell and J. C. Hamlett were the entrepreneurs most responsible for the development of the prestigious northeastern portion of the city's Tampa Bay shoreline, beginning in 1911.

Snell contributed to the creation of a system of waterfront parks running north from Central Avenue to the entrance of Snell Isle, a mangrove island he transformed into an elite island development in the first years of the 1920s. Dredging Coffee Pot Bayou, he increased the land mass of the island lying between the north shore of St. Petersburg and Tampa Bay. He opened a golf course on the island and constructed a clubhouse in 1920 described in the *St. Petersburg Times* as evidencing "the ornate mélange of Moorish or Spanish Renaissance influences Snell so favored-minarets, heavily bracketed cornices, 'keyhole arches' and onion domes." Snell and his competitor, Howard Schooley, built speculative homes designed by noted Mediterranean-revival architects, including Kiehnel, on Snell Isle and the stretch of shore paralleling Coffee Pot Boulevard that is now known as Historic Old Northeast.

Kiehnel also designed the Rolyat Hotel, a handsome establishment intended to resemble a Spanish walled settlement of the feudal ages, which opened with champagne flowing from its central fountain in 1926. Two other grand hotels debuted as St. Petersburg teetered on the brink of the Florida land boom's collapse. The Vinoy Park Hotel opened in 1926 on Tampa Bay, a pink stucco confection with frothy white cast stone detail. The Don CeSar graced St. Petersburg Beach two years later, a pink castlelike structure that, like the Vinoy, revealed an unrestrained mixture of Spanish and Moorish detail. Both hotels boasted massive and masculine public rooms, the Vinoy's decorated with stenciled pecky cypress beams and frescoed walls and ceilings, and the Don CeSar's with marble floors and Spanish tile. Both were transformed into military facilities within fifteen years, and have survived, refurbished as luxury hotels, into the present.

These and many other hotels, planned communities, and development schemes met their communal fate in the mid-1920s. It took a combination of manmade factors, in the form of increased scrutiny and criticism from the government, media, and financial institutions; a railroad embargo slowing shipment of building materials; a shipwreck blocking access to Miami Harbor; and natural forces, in the shape of a destructive hurricane, to pop the bubble that year. An even more deadly hurricane in 1928 and the nationwide depression that descended the following year ended any hopes that the boom was experiencing only a temporary lull. Although Florida never lost its popularity as a winter destination and began to resume growth in more measured fashion in the 1930s, by that time architectural tastes had shifted. Modernism had come to America, and the picturesque, romantic aspect of Spanish and Mediterranean revival–style architecture appeared quaint and old-fashioned compared to the streamlined forms characterizing the Art Deco style.

However, neither architects nor their patrons fully abandoned the style that had become so fully associated with the tropical climate and relaxed yet elegant lifestyle of the state's resort towns. Many architects found that the language of Spanish and Mediterranean architecture adapted easily to the rhythmic geometry and severe linearity

Opposite: High relief door and window surrounds invoke the Churrigueresque mode of Spanish Baroque design, lending frothy appeal to the pastel edifice of the Reniassance Vinoy.

Overleaf: Constructed as Florida's land boom collapsed, the Don Cesar is both literally and metaphorically a castle built upon the sand, its pink and white towers tossing a challenge to the fates of time and change.

Opposite and Above: Domestic architecture in St. Petersburg displays a range of Mediterranean influences, from severe Spanish-style homes to more fanciful edifices, including this house and gazebo designed for Howard Schooley on Snell Isle.

of modern design, creating homes and commercial properties that blended Old and New World styles. Others, like Gamble Rogers, who worked primarily in the inland resort and college town of Winter Park, found plentiful patrons still desirous of romantic, revivalist-style homes. During the 1930s, Rogers built numerous homes inspired by Spanish country farmhouses, and the president of Rollins College selected the Spanish style as the unifying architectural idiom of the growing school.

As the twentieth century ended, and the next millennium began, the style experienced a full-scale revival, with huge Spanish, Italian, and French Mediterranean–inspired mansions cropping up along the southern coast from South Carolina to Florida.

Ironically, many of these mansions are being built upon the foundations of preexisting ones in similar styles, deemed too small or too old-fashioned for modern living. But many more of these increasingly prized historic structures are being preserved as Floridians realize that they form one of their greatest cultural achievements: the articulation of a unique architectural style that reflects their state's history and responds to its natural environment.

In her introduction to the 1928 publication *Florida Architecture of Addison Mizner*, journalist Ida M. Tarbell described the view from the top floor of the architect's tower residence in Palm Beach. "Look out from Mizner's window and see the true Florida skyline—those red tiled roofs, peaked, variable, at different elevations, and all at such a height that the thing which makes the most beauty against the sky in all of Florida, the palm, receives its full value."[22]

Writing from Coral Gables in 1925, Price similarly observed the appropriateness of the Spanish style of architecture to the Florida setting, as well as its practicality. "The Mediterranean style of architecture, which will probably more often be called 'Spanish,' as it becomes more widely known throughout the country, is one that is naturally in harmony with the tropical trees and flowers, and with Florida skies, and the cool, arcaded loggias and patios are not only picturesque, but are essentials of comfortable living in warm climates."[23] The preservation and perpetuation of this architectural tradition, as illustrated in the following pages exploring seventeen residences constructed between the years 1921 and 2001, reveal the enduring truth of this prescient declaration.

~

NOTES

1. *Florida: The American Guide Series* (New York: Oxford University Press, 1939), p. 48.

2. Jose M. Lozano, "The Last Eclectics: Walter De Garmo and Richard Kiehnel in South Florida," *SECAC Review* (1990): p. 363.

3. Albert Manucy, *The Houses of St. Augustine* (St. Augustine, Fla.: St. Augustine Historical Society, 1978), p. 8.

4. William Stark, *An Account of East Florida, with a Journal Kept by John Bartram of Philadelphia, Botanist to His Majesty for the Floridas: Upon a Journey from St. Augustine up the River St. Johns* (London: Nicholl & Woodfall, 1769).

5. David Nolan, *The Houses of St. Augustine* (Sarasota, Fla.: Pineapple Press, 1995), p. 48.

6. Rexford Newcomb, *Mediterranean Domestic Architecture in the United States* (Cleveland, Ohio: J. H. Hansen, 1928), p. 4.

7. Nolan, p. 46.

8. Les Standiford, *Last Train to Paradise* (New York: Crown, 2002), p. 48.

9. Ibid., p. 54.

10. *Florida*, p. 287.

11. Donald Curl, *Mizner's Florida* (New York: Architectural History Foundation and Cambridge, Massachusetts, and London: MIT Press, 1984), p. 42.

12. Ibid., p. 42.

13. Caroline Seebohm, *Boca Rococo* (New York: Clarkson Potter, 2001), p. 163.

14. Christina Orr, *Addison Mizner, Architect of Dreams and Realities* (Palm Beach, Fla.: Norton Art Gallery, Society of the Four Arts, The Henry Morrison Flagler Museum, and The Historical Society of Palm Beach County, 1977), pp. 19–20.

15. Quoted in Seebohm, p. 163.

16. Mary Fanton Roberts, "Cielito Lindo," *Arts & Decoration* 9, no. 3 (July 1928): n.p.

17. Orr, p. 38.

18. Curl, p. 134.

19. Curl, p. 135.

20. Matlack Price, "Coral Gables-Miami," *Arts & Decoration* (January 1925): p. 2.

21. Florida, p. 262.

22. Quoted in Curl, p. xli.

23. Price, p. 5.

Buenos Recuerdos

A 1927 Spanish-Style Villa in Palm Beach

THE HOME OF MRS. WILLIAM ORR

The Spanish-style villas built on Palm Beach in the 1920s were designed as winter homes for seasonal residents from northern climes who came to enjoy the languid breezes that bathed the tropical isle throughout the year. Informed by the style Addison Mizner popularized through the sensational Everglades Club, these dwellings wrapped long arms around central courtyards lined with deep loggias. This form offered a progression of spaces: the roofless "room" of the patio, the open-walled spaces of the colonnades, and well-ventilated interior rooms where windows on two and even three sides invited the easy flow of air and light. The indoor-outdoor way of living these houses encouraged, inspired by southern Mediterranean and North African regions, offered a novel lifestyle, at once practical and romantic, that delighted Palm Beach denizens.

With the advent of air-conditioning, whose impact upon architecture can be compared only with that of the automobile and airplane upon modern transportation, these houses, in their original state, became endangered species. Many residents decided to enjoy their houses year-round, employing air-conditioning to cool rooms never intended for use during the hottest months of the year. The outdoor living rooms and hallways afforded by the long colonnades became impractical, so many residents began enclosing them, sometimes gracefully, but often with awkward windows that destroyed the elegant proportions and obscured the majestic detail of the cloisterlike spaces. Many grand Spanish-style mansions fell to the wrecking ball as home owners decided to build anew in architectural styles better suited to the air-conditioned lifestyle pervading Palm Beach.

For these reasons, a house such as Buenos Recuerdos, designed in 1927 by renowned architect Maurice Fatio for Mr. and Mrs. Henry G. Barkausen, and sold in 1938 to its present-day owner, who has never modified the structure, survives as a Rosetta stone for understanding the classic Palm Beach lifestyle. Like her predecessors, Mrs. Orr has always considered the house a winter residence, maintaining the traditional season that stretches from late December through early May. She and her first husband, Abram Nesbitt, both of Pennsylvania, began wintering in Palm Beach in the mid-1930s. They rented a series of

Opposite: With a massive ogee-arched doorway and three-story tower, Buenos Recuerdos, designed by Fatio in 1927, presents a street-side facade that is at once fanciful and formidable.

A seventeen-foot ceiling with decorative beams arranged in an Islamic star motif crowns the massive stair hall that opens into two of the house's three loggias, as well as a small private library and large living room. Original iron light fixtures and furnishings complement the Spanish-revival setting.

Opposite: *The wide spaces and decorative details consistent with the interior of the house—glazed tile floors and cypress ceilings—clearly communicate the architect's intention that this colonnade be used as a semi-enclosed living room.*

Spanish revival–style houses, including Buenos Recuerdos, whose owners, financially ruined by the 1929 stock market collapse, sold them the house in 1938.

The house came with many of its furnishings in place, including a number of pieces manufactured in Mizner's Los Manos factory. Despite the fact that it was only eleven years old when it changed hands, the house's contents already showed signs of decay indicative of Palm Beach's Depression-era decline. "The lamp shades were getting to shreds," Mrs. Orr recalls. However, the essential bones of the house were in fine shape, and an architect friend of the Nesbitts said, "For goodness's sake, buy it. It's a very good house."

Mrs. Orr, now in her nineties, agrees. "It's just been a wonderful house," she says. "I like the outdoors of it, the way it opens up." In the fifty-seven years that she has lived in the house with Mr. Nesbitt and, following his death, her second husband, William Orr,

she and her family have enjoyed the comfortable, casually elegant lifestyle the house so perfectly accommodates.

Unlike many of the Spanish-style houses influenced by Mizner's characteristic approach, which marries the interior focus on traditional Spanish courtyard dwellings with the facade-oriented decoration beloved by America's wealthy, Buenos Recuerdos offers an austere, almost fortresslike facade to the street. The long masonry wall features a tall ogee-arched doorway set with an imposing wood door studded with nails. A window above is covered with a wrought-iron grille, as are the side windows that flank the front door.

When the heavy front door creaks open, visitors make a delightful transition from this imposing facade to an interior filled with spaces that draw them into the heart of the house. Standing in a white stucco entrance hall crowned with beams of pecky cypress, they look through the white-painted filigree of a wrought-iron gate and a procession of arched openings into the sun-filled courtyard. Across the verdant expanse, a shady arcade supported by delicate Gothic columns and surmounted by a roof of warm red barrel tiles offers a picturesque vista. Passing through the filigree gates, guests find themselves in one of three colonnades that enclose the courtyard (the fourth wall masks the service area), linking dining, living, and sleeping quarters.

To the right is a stately dining room with a soaring ceiling of pecky cypress beams stretching above a floor clad in cool clay tiles. In reaction to the dark and cluttered décor of the previously popular Victorian styles, rooms such as these required minimal decoration in the way of floor and wall coverings. No carpet covers the floor, and the only ornamentation on the white stucco walls are the carved cypress mantelpiece and paneled cypress doors that open onto the entrance loggia on one side and a breakfast porch on the other. Tall windows

The living room's original tile floors, stenciled cypress ceiling beams, and iron chandeliers perpetuate the elegant austerity that was the hallmark of Spanish-revival interiors.

46

Opposite: High ceilings and apertures in all four walls ensure cool, comfortable conditions in this dining room, which retains not only its original decorative details, but also reproduction Spanish-style furnishings attributed to Mizner's Los Manos factory.

Left: This bronze chair, with its fraying tapestry and velvet upholstery, is attributed to Mizner's Los Manos factory, which provided decorative details and furnishings to many of the island's wealthy residents.

bring light and air into the room, with simple Fortuny silk draperies whose terra-cotta and grisaille palette match the earthy color scheme of the room. A long dining table with wavy slat-backed chairs in the Spanish style and massive sideboards, purportedly designed by Mizner, are the room's original furnishings.

During the annual Christmas cocktail dinner held at Buenos Recuerdos, an inviting buffet greets visitors in this room. After serving themselves, guests stroll out into the many semienclosed spaces that wrap around the courtyard where a well, surrounded by grape trees and hibiscus plants, completes the picturesque Spanish mood. Designed for entertaining, the house also features an oversized enclosed entrance hall to the left of the front door, which rises seventeen feet high and is crowned by a cypress ceiling decorated with an Islamic star motif. Forming the base of a three-story stair tower, this hallway opens directly onto two loggias as well as a cavernous living room.

At one end of the living room, a small barroom lined with pecky cypress walls attests to the stylish hospitality architects kept in mind when designing Palm Beach mansions. On the far side of the room, which is crowned by stenciled cypress beams and illuminated

An octagonal fountain with colorful patterned tiles and a
wrought-iron pulley offers a picturesque Iberian touch to the
very Spanish courtyard.

Opposite: *In contrast to the exterior, the walls facing the
courtyard are open and inviting, with varied window types and
colonnade treatments blurring the boundaries between indoor
and outdoor spaces.*

by massive iron chandeliers, stands a large fireplace bracketed by niches set into the white
stucco walls. Bridge tables cluster at one end of the room on top of a carpet laid across
original tile floors. Tall French doors open onto a shaded colonnade, where wicker chairs
piled deep with cushions in tropical tones provide a less formal retreat.

A master bedroom suite extends above the living room, its windows and balcony
affording views of the courtyard and surrounding neighborhood, and a third-story
belvedere in the top floor of the stair tower claims vistas of the Atlantic Ocean and Lake
Worth. Four more bedrooms designed for guests and children complete the house's
accommodations—all opening off the intimate Gothic cloister-style colonnade opposite
the arched entrance.

Whether raising her son, hosting her annual Christmas party, entertaining her grand-
daughter, Geraldine Nesbitt, with her daughter and dogs, or enjoying quiet hours on her
own, Mrs. Orr explains that the house has perfectly met the many demands of Palm
Beach living. "I just love being in it," she declares.

The DeGarmo Estate

A 1921 Courtyard Villa in Coconut Grove, Miami

THE HOME OF JOHN ROETTGER
AND BRIAN MOLLOY

From its earliest days, Coconut Grove has attracted intellectuals, artists, writers, adventurers, and high-minded escapists. Among Miami's earliest villages (but not officially a part of Miami until the mid-1920s—and even then incorporated against its residents' will), it was first settled by Charles Peacock, who came from London in 1875 to visit his brother, "Jolly Jack" Peacock. Jack Peacock "kept the House of Refuge established by the government for shipwrecked sailors over in the wilds of Miami Beach," according to a history of Miami written by Helen Muir.[1] Muir claims that the first sight of the area to become known as Coconut Grove "sent Charles Peacock's stout heart to the bottom of his English boots."

Charles and Isabella first settled at the mouth of the Miami River, where several other Florida pioneers, including William Brickel, were already ensconced. After seven years, they moved to the area now known as Coconut Grove and built Peacock Inn, a small house covered with shingles made from the foremast of a wrecked brig and equipped with a porch overlooking Biscayne Bay. There, Isabella supervised a table laid with excellent meals, rooms were let (along with meals) for ten dollars a week, and sailboats were rented for two dollars a day.[2]

Before long, the Peacocks had expanded the inn to accommodate a growing number of visitors, who included adventure-story author Kirk Munroe; Mary Barr Munroe, whose mother wrote *Remember the Alamo*; Charles Stowe, son of Harriet Beecher Stowe; and Ralph Munroe. Known as the Commodore, Ralph Munroe made a study of local plant life and fishing conditions. After a visit to Peacock House, Mrs. Andrew Carnegie was so impressed by the intellectual quality of the tropical outpost that she sent enough books to start the Coconut Grove Library.

It was into this cultivated wilderness that former Swarthmore College president Charles DeGarmo and his son, successful New York architect Walter DeGarmo, came in 1903, at the urging of their friend, botanist Dr. John Gifford. When Walter DeGarmo opened his Miami office in 1904, there were only two other architects listed in the city

Opposite: The 1921 house that DeGarmo designed for his family in Coconut Grove offers a rather formidable facade that encloses a large cloistered courtyard in its center.

directory, both of whom specialized in late-Victorian styles.[3] DeGarmo, who had completed formal training at Cornell University and practiced within the Beaux Arts tradition under New York's John Russell Pope, brought loftier Classical ideals with him to Miami, as well as an interest in developing a regionally inspired tropical architecture. The first registered architect in Miami, his contributions are impressive, including the Miami City Hall in 1901 (now demolished) and, in collaboration with other key architects of Coral Gables, the Colonnade Building and the Douglas Entrance to the Gables.

DeGarmo's interest in marrying the antique vocabulary of Beaux Arts design with an architecture responsive to Florida's landscape and climate found full expression in the Coconut Grove house he built for his family in 1921. Nestled amid dense tropical growth, the house of steel-reinforced concrete reveals combined influences of Roman, Moorish, and Spanish design. "Wherever people come from, including my cousin who lives in Egypt," says current resident John Roettger, "they say the house reminds them of home." Perhaps this is because the house draws upon one of the most ancient and ubiquitous forms: the quadrangular courtyard.

The facade of the house presents a long masonry wall penetrated by five arched openings and terminating in a projecting bay framing a tall, rectangular door. Fitted with decorative wrought-iron grills, the arches open into a covered arcade that forms one wall of an enclosed courtyard. Two wings on either side accommodate lofty entertaining rooms with colorful tile floors and windows in three walls. The rear wall of the courtyard originally formed a second open-air arcade that paralleled the dining room at the rear of the house and connected the two side wings. "All this hallway that is floored with terra-cotta tile was originally outdoor space," says Mr. Roettger. "You had to walk outdoors to get from room to room."

Previous: The dining room, floored with marble, features a large pair of bifold wood doors, original to the house, which once gave onto an open-air arcade facing the courtyard.

Left: The long living room parallels the courtyard. Its floor is paved with imported tile, original to the house, and its ceiling beams are made from molded concrete painted to resemble wood.

59

Although previous residents made this concession to modern-day air-conditioning, the enclosed arcade does not undermine the appearance of the courtyard and improves the flow of traffic inside the house. Mr. Roettger and his partner, Brian Molloy, have dedicated their efforts to restoring DeGarmo's house as much as possible to its original appearance. According to Mr. Molloy, the house showed signs of significant decay when they purchased it, including deterioration of the living room's walls and ceiling. The richly tiled floors and walls were badly in need of cleaning, and the walls were dark with age. But still, says Mr. Molloy, "every other house we saw paled in comparison to the architecture of this house, the grandness of the rooms, the lovely courtyard, the sense of openness, and the light that comes in."

Mr. Roettger and Mr. Molloy first moved to Coconut Grove from Coral Gables in 1983, attracted by the same combination of untamed tropical landscape and free-thinking intellectualism that had appealed to DeGarmo. "We really feel like we belong in the Grove," says Mr. Molloy. "It's a little more bohemian and laid-back than Coral Gables, which is more manicured and conservative."

There is certainly nothing manicured about the house's natural setting, which is overgrown with bougainvillea and includes a deep sunken garden. A manmade waterfall cascades into the natural depression that is technically known as a solution pit. Created over hundreds of years by the leaching of tannic acid from fallen leaves and the cavities left by decaying tree roots, the limestone cavern creates a dramatic landscape element behind the house. While previous owners had attempted to fill it in with soil, Mr. Roettger and Mr. Molloy excavated it and installed the waterfall. "We often have hors d'oeuvres or after-dinner drinks down there during parties," says Mr. Molloy, whose niece Kayla and nephew Liam enjoy roasting marshmallows over a fire pit there during winter visits.

Festive entertainments have long been held at the house, which was built on a plot of land where three generations of the DeGarmo family lived. During the 1950s, it was the site of frequent Tom and Jerry parties, bibulous events featuring the popular cocktail of that name. "I've met many people who have attended parties at this house," Mr. Molloy reports. Whether hosting neighborhood get-togethers or meetings of the Coconut Grove Garden Club or enjoying quiet hours in the cool embrace the house's rooms, the current residents find their eighty-five-year-old house to be as practical as it is beautiful. "We can't imagine living anywhere else," says Mr. Roettger.

NOTES

1. Helen Muir, *Miami, U.S.A.* (Miami: Pickering Press, 1953), p. 25.

2. Ibid., p. 26.

3. Margot Ammidown, "Walter DeGarmo: Fantasies in Concrete," *Update: Historical Association of South Florida 2*, no. 10 (February 1984): p. 4.

Casita Collage

A Circa-1920 West Palm Beach Casita

HOME OF BRUCE AND CLAUDIA HELANDER

Internationally celebrated collage artist Bruce Helander "has the instincts of a magpie and the energy of a carnival pitchman," writes Henry Geldzahler in his introduction to *Curious Collage*. These two urges are immediately apparent when Mr. Helander conducts a tour of the 1920s Spanish-style casita he and his wife, Claudia, purchased six years ago. "We planned an engaging, animated entrance that used cut coral stone as an introduction to the historic quality of the house," he explains. "Then we put in a turn-of-the-century iron gate, never painted, just the way it was, so it also gave the feeling of entering into an old world. Then, we added a series of steps to give the sensation that you are moving up to something. As you move through the first gate, and approach the second one, you naturally look up at the three-story house, which seems taller than it actually is."

This masterminded approach combines a collection of materials that express Florida's history—cut coral stone that was one of the state's earliest building materials, old wrought iron that harkens back to its Spanish colonization, and railroad ties that evoke the role modern transportation played in transforming the state into a vacation mecca. Lush tree ferns exude the primeval quality of the tropical region's indigenous flora. A stockade fence laminated with a collage featuring tiny figures surrounded by oversized butterflies and flowers introduces an element of whimsy that pervades the retreat enjoyed by Mr. Helander and his wife, a floral designer who also assists in the construction of his collages.

The couple found the house while searching for a home that both complemented their aesthetic and was large enough to house their ever-growing collection of art and flea market finds. When they found the circa-1920s Spanish casita, it had recently been moved from a previous location, losing windows and doors in the process, and had suffered a fire that left many of its interior surfaces blackened and charred. Yet the Helanders were struck by the unexpectedly grand proportions of the house's entrance tower and living room and the ruined vestiges of Spanish splendor.

Opposite: A collagelike layering of iron gates, coral stone steps, and railroad ties leads to the front door of the Helanders' 1920s casita in West Palm Beach—hinting at the old-Florida quality of the house beyond.

The burnished expanse of a pecky cypress ceiling, once charred black in a fire and subsequently sandblasted, gives the living room of this modest house a castlelike aura. Found objects, contemporary art, and antique furnishings provide a fanciful setting.

Opposite: *Exotic eclecticism reigns in the entrance hall, where the decorative details of Moorish doors, an Indian altar, and an Italian marble tabletop (transformed into a colorful welcome mat) mingle congenially.*

One of the first things the Helanders did was to sandblast the ceilings, revealing the original pecky cypress beams. They tracked down salvaged doors and windows, including a Moroccan-style arched front door as well as a carved door surround and stained-glass window for the living room. They paved the floors, which had been clad in unattractive white ceramic tile, with earthy Mexican tiles and discovered a colorful cut-marble Italian tabletop, which they placed on the floor of the entrance hall.

Mr. Helander had been eyeing the piece for some time in an antiques store. "One day, I walked in and it was gone," he recalls. "The proprietor explained that one of his customers had backed into it and broken it into about fifty pieces. So instead of a $7,500 tabletop, it was a steal at fifty bucks." The collage artist reassembled it, transforming it into a welcome mat that reflects the mélange of Italian, Spanish, and Moorish elements that characterize Florida's Mediterranean-revival style.

An Indian altarpiece adds another exotic element to the foyer, while vintage table-cloths printed with bright Floridiana prints flutter from windows lining the stairs. The entrance hall leads to the living room, a cavernous space that is densely populated with furniture and art. "You have a beautiful ceiling and floor, and in between a balance of things that work with both, some of which are very elegant, and some, very rustic," Mr. Helander explains. He points out a gilded trumeau mirror hanging above a refined double-chest and a two-hundred-year-old Canadian altar table covered with flickering candles. "Neither my wife nor I are particularly religious, but Claudia comes from Colombia, where they are very interested in *spiritos*. We thought this would be our little spirit table."

Found objects, including an old farm implement for sharpening tools, share space with fine art, including a painting entitled *Turtle Chair* by Alfonse Borysewicz that hangs above the mantel and a cartoonish lamp in the shape of a cat's face by Stevan Jennis framed by the fireplace. A set design created by Mr. Helander hangs above the sofa, its surface embellished with arches and trellises that provide the illusion of entering a garden. Beside the painting is a door that frames an actual view of the surrounding garden and leads to an outdoor sitting room. An arcade set beneath a pecky cypress ceiling, the space is a typical pre-air-conditioning Florida sitting room that is one of the couple's favorite haunts.

A door opening off the opposite side of the living room leads to the dining room, a square room dominated by a rustic wardrobe painted green. "This green is so engaging, so magical, so luminous," exclaims Mr. Helander, who adds that he and his wife search for furnishings that "we know we can have forever, and we're not worried if anyone spills anything or chips anything—they just get better with age. Like the house, these things are full of life, full of breath, just wonderful, fun things to have."

Brightly colored objects and surfaces abound in the dining room, adjacent kitchen, and Florida room: green storm shutters removed from a Palm Beach mansion and transformed into a sideboard and kitchen cabinets; linoleum, circa 1920, designed for a child's room; a wall of stained-glass panels. "We found four empty window panels with such a good look to them, with almost Asian proportions to the mullions," recalls Mr. Helander. "Then I called a stained-glass company and asked them to give me sixty pieces of glass, all assorted, with as much texture and color as possible." This assemblage created a jewel-toned glass wall that divides the kitchen from the Florida room.

Adding further animation to the décor are the couple's collections of objects ranging from salt and pepper shakers to English cups and teapots, all decorated with faces, and three-dimensional industrial sculpture from the Golden Age of advertising. "This little guy is the rarest of the rare," Mr. Helander says, indicating a papier-mâché sculpture of the Porter Paint man, designed to hold a quart of paint in his outstretched hand. In the kitchen, a widely smiling lady clad in a white apron advertises Westinghouse home appliances, while a large lemon with green legs and red shoes promotes lemon liqueur.

Previous: A collection of salt and pepper shakers from the 1930s, '40s, and '50s displayed in a glass-front cupboard in the dining room all reveal tiny visages, whether a human face, animal face, or a fruit or flower face. A Porter Paint company advertising figure, clad in bright orange overalls and hat, stands in the corner.

Opposite: An old worktable supports several of the Helanders' collection of advertising figures, whose bright colors are echoed by the stained-glass wall dividing the kitchen from the Florida room.

A two-hundred-year-old Canadian candle altar surrounded by religious artifacts including a contemporary leaning cross sculpture by Michael Price and a stained-glass window, evoke the ecclesiastical influence common in Spanish-style architecture and design.

Opposite: *Stately Corinthian columns and a pecky cypress ceiling lend a sense of grandeur and elegance to this small side porch.*

Mr. Helander's collecting habit began in the 1970s when, as an art student at the Rhode Island School of Design, he befriended glass artist and flea market devotee Dale Chihuly. "I was immediately captivated by the wit and whimsy of these little things," he says of the salt and pepper shakers with which Mr. Helander launched his own collection. Now he and Mrs. Helander haunt flea markets regularly, searching not only for objects for their home but also raw materials for the artist's collages and commercial designs. "Adaptively reusing these materials in a collage format is what really excites me and keeps me interested in what I'm doing," exclaims the artist. Texture, color, wit, time, and space—these, according to Mr. Helander, are the elements of successful collages, as well as the ingredients of the perfect home.

House of Tiles

A 1922 Spanish-Style Villa in Palm Beach

THE HOME OF MAHNAZ AND JOHN WHELTON

The house that Marion Sims Wyeth designed in 1922 for New York stockbroker J. F. Carlisle is an example of Palm Beach's Spanish style at its best. Blending elegant ecclesiastical details inspired by pre-Baroque Spanish architecture with the irregular massing and decorative exuberance of Andalusian residences in southern Spain, it balances the formal with the informal, creating an ideal vacation home designed for both relaxed retreat and elegant entertaining. Located on Golf View Road, the house now inhabited by Mahnaz and John Whelton was, and still is, considered one of the most desirable properties on the island, thanks in part to proximity to the Everglades Club and Worth Avenue shopping area, which form the stylistic and communal heart of the island.

Worth Avenue and Golf View Road were among the first areas to be developed by Paris Singer, the sewing machine scion who came to Palm Beach in 1918, according to a brief history of the neighborhood compiled by the Garden Club of Palm Beach in 2000. Architect Addison Mizner, then based in New York, joined his friend and soon-to-be business partner later that year. He remained, becoming a major architectural visionary, as well as a colorful figure on the social scene.

Singer first built a club (originally designated as a convalescent home for returning World War I soldiers before becoming the Everglades Club), designed by Mizner, and then a golf course. Residential lots overlooking the course were laid out along Golf View Road. Nearby Worth Avenue was developed with a mix of residential and commercial properties. Marion Sims Wyeth, who had enjoyed a successful career at the New York architectural firm of Carrère & Hastings, came south to partake in the building boom in Palm Beach in 1919. After designing the first home on Golf View Road, he was invited to design several more along the fairway, all in Mediterranean revival styles.

The home Wyeth designed for Carlisle included not only the large structure now inhabited by the Wheltons, but also an adjacent one linked by a loggia, which was divided in 1949 to form a separate residence. At that time, a large shared courtyard was transformed into the driveway and parking area by which the Wheltons' house is approached.

Opposite: This loggia, with fern-shaped capitals, a pecky cypress beamed ceiling, and Spanish tile floor, once connected the Wheltons' house with the structure next door, which was originally part of the house Wyeth designed for New York stockbroker J. F. Carlisle.

Paved with brick and painted Spanish tile, this court leads to two entrances, one tucked beneath the loggia, which is decorated with Roman arches and cast stone columns, and the other, up a small flight of stairs flanked by cast stone elephants and lions. This discreet entrance, which allowed visitors to enter the house without the knowledge of house servants, is rumored to have been created for the convenience of secret paramours.

Andalusian details abound in the entrance court, including colorful tiles embedded in textured stucco walls and the exterior stair. A variety of window and door styles, including Roman arches, ogee arches, and rectangular casement windows with iron grills, add more visual interest to the polyrhythmic space. Upon entering the space (most guests enter through the door of heavy cast iron and plate glass that lies hidden at the end of the loggia), guests encounter the playful variation of light and space that also characterizes Andalusian design.

From the bright expanse of the entrance court, residents and guests step into the shade of the

Above and Opposite: While the Spanish tile laid out in the courtyard creates the illusion of a giant oriental carpet unfurled upon the ground, tile borders outlining the exterior stair add a Jazz Age rhythm to the facade of the house.

Overleaf: The beams and brackets of the pecky cypress ceiling in the living room had been hidden by white plaster cloth for decades. The Wheltons removed it in an effort to restore the Spanish baronial character of the room.

loggia, where a pecky cypress ceiling and cool tile floors offer respite from the sun. Passing through the front door, they find themselves in a small transitional space with white stucco walls and colorful tile floors and window surrounds. Beyond beckons a long stair hall with a large arched opening ushering them into the cavernous space of the living room. An open-beamed ceiling of pecky cypress soars above, and a floor, now clad in white marble, spreads across the space to windows overlooking the golf course at the front of the house and an arcade, once open to a side court, to the left.

Although the basic character and decorative details of the original house have remained relatively unchanged, subsequent owners have modified some aspects. At one point, after the Spanish style fell from favor, a former resident covered the living room ceiling with white plaster cloth and installed white marble floors. It was probably the same owner who enclosed the colonnade paralleling the living room with sliding glass doors. The Wheltons uncovered the original wood ceiling and redesigned the colonnade, which, though still enclosed, now features more appropriate arched windows.

While restoring the original Andalusian style to the living room, the Wheltons have added their own decorative motifs, using an eclectic style that draws from Mrs. Whelton's Iranian ancestry and Mr. Whelton's European heritage. A large Persian carpet covers the floor; artwork by French and English masters (including Joshua Reynolds) adorns the

Opposite: Colorful painted tiles are used liberally within and without the house. These original tiles are of Spanish origin, made to order for Palm Beach's architects, while Persian tiles collected by Mrs. Whelton can be found in other parts of the house.

Above: A loggia, once open to a courtyard, is now enclosed, forming a second dining room running parallel to the house's original dining room.

walls. French, Italian, and English furniture, some exhibiting the influence of Chinese and Japanese design, elegantly furnish the room, complemented by a contemporary table of plate glass balanced on a floral jardinière.

In the stair hall, the Wheltons have added another transcultural detail: a large tile mosaic featuring a courtier on horseback. This work of highly refined Renaissance Persian tile was purchased at auction from the Hearst Estate. Standing at the foot of the stair hall, the courtier seems to beckon toward the dining room at the rear of the house. Here, another Persian carpet covers the marble floor and an Elizabethan sideboard stretches across one wall. While the chairs surrounding the table are European antiques, a mix of sixteenth- and eighteenth-century French chairs, the table is made of beveled glass and Lucite. "The chairs are so light in design that I wanted the table to seem to float in the middle of them," Mrs. Whelton explains.

The original dining room is paralleled by another loggia with Roman arches supported above columns with cast stone capitals adorned with seahorses. Originally designed as an exterior arcade facing a courtyard garden, the structure was enclosed with the addition of

Laid out by a master tiler, the kitchen's counters and walls are decorated with a combination of Spanish and Persian tiles. A Persian lamp hangs above the long tiled island that is often used for family meals or informal buffet-style dinners.

Opposite: *Dating from the fifteenth or sixteenth century, this mosaic panel of Persian tile was purchased by the Wheltons at auction from the Hearst Estate.*

a family sitting room on the far side. Now the interior arcade serves as a second dining area for small parties or when a large gathering is too large for the main dining room alone. The sun-filled family sitting room overlooks the swimming pool, added in the 1930s, through a wall of windows.

The Wheltons made their own modifications to the house, transforming an area of service rooms into a large kitchen, where they continued their aesthetic of blending Spanish and Persian details. On a trip to Iran, Mrs. Whelton discovered a trove of antique Persian tiles in an area as renowned for its tile making as Toledo. She brought these back to Palm Beach and combined them with a cache of Toledo tiles made for and imported by Addison Mizner that she and her husband discovered in boxes beneath the house. These form the decorative details of the spacious kitchen, which is ideal for family dining and informal entertainments.

Including the tiles that are original to the house and those added by the Wheltons, the house may feature more decorative tile per square foot than any other in Palm Beach. The decorative motif continues in the four tiled courtyards that surround the house. A small courtyard beyond the kitchen features a fountain tiled with a scene of the Virgin and child. Another, enclosed between the kitchen and a two-story guest quarters, features blue and white tiles from Spain, which line the risers of an exterior stair, and Turkish tiles with arabesque letters.

Vines and blossoms cascade from balconies and roof gardens, and tropical plants cluster in shady corners, filling the courtyards with the sweet-spicy scent of frangipani and the scattered blossoms of bougainvillea. Giant tree ferns, orchids, jungle ferns, traveler palms, and giant begonia grow in profusion, alternating cool green foliage with colorful blooms. "This house has a very young, happy feeling, with a perfect balance of the formal and informal," Mrs. Whelton muses. "We use every part of it. There are courtyards where I can garden, and large rooms where we entertain. And the location—we love to walk to Worth Avenue," she continues, listing the house's virtues—virtues that made it one of Palm Beach's most desirable homes nearly a century ago and that still contribute to its allure today.

Villa Mizner

A 1924 Tower Residence on Via Mizner in Palm Beach

THE FORMER HOME OF ADDISON MIZNER

It is not surprising that architect Addison Mizner created the ultimate fantasy house for himself—not just the house of his dreams, but a "vertical palace"[1] rising within the city of his dreams: Villa Mizner on Via Mizner. The tower rises five stories high, with shops below to showcase his furnishings and decorative designs, a gargantuan living room with a fireplace rumored to be large enough to accommodate ten men, and a terrace where his chows, birds, and monkeys could frolic above Worth Avenue.

The entertainments Mizner hosted there were legendary, including a two-week spate during which the New York String Quartet played daily into sunset. "They sat in the middle of the great Gothic room, with the lights on their music stands as the only illumination, and played divinely, as daylight died through the soft tints of the colored glass," Mizner later wrote. "People came in quietly, without greetings, and sank into big chairs, and one felt medieval as the footman stole about lighting great cathedral candles here and there."

The progenitor of Palm Beach's Spanish style, Mizner drew upon his direct experience of Spanish Colonial and Mediterranean architecture and urban design. As a teenager, he traveled extensively in Central America while his father, Lansing Mizner, served as minister plenipotentiary to the states of Guatemala, Honduras, El Salvador, Nicaragua, and Costa Rica. Mizner described his first view of a Spanish town in Mexico, "lying white in the sun," as "probably the greatest day of my life." After a brief but adventurous jaunt as a Yukon gold miner, Mizner returned to Guatemala, having retooled himself as a coffee importer. Instead of importing coffee, however, he shipped an entire Antiguan monastery back to New York, along with a scrapbook filled with photographs and sketches of Colonial palaces and churches and Baroque city scenes. Finally, in his twenties, Addison traveled to Spain, Morocco, and Italy, where he rounded out his exposure to the Mediterranean roots of the Colonial architecture he had come to love.

The fullness of this experience bore fruit in downtown Palm Beach, where Worth Avenue became lined on one side by Mizner's wildly popular Everglades Club and on the

Opposite: Viewed from a first-floor balcony on the far side of Via Mizner, Villa Mizner assumes a picturesque silhouette evocative of antique towns in southern Spain.

This bridge over Via Parigi, possibly influenced by the Bridge of Sighs, connected Villa Mizner with the three-story office building the architect constructed to house his workshop and studio. It complements the romantic, irregular arrangement of spaces Mizner envisioned for Via Mizner and Via Parigi.

Opposite: Doors of heavily studded cypress offer a formidable welcome to the ground-level entrance foyer of Villa Mizner, while a wrought-iron gate on the opposite side lets in light and air.

other by Via Mizner and Via Parigi, a miniature medieval Mediterranean city filled with irregular pedestrian walks, overhung with bridges and balconies, and opening out into sun-filled courtyards. Having been driven out of residence in the Everglades Club by new regulations banning animals on the premises and ladies above the first floor, Mizner began his quest to find a permanent home. After building several exquisite Spanish-style villas in the untamed outer jungles of Palm Beach—which were quickly snapped up by wealthy clients—he returned to the center of the community.

First Mizner constructed a three-story office building opposite the Everglades Club, including a studio, a showroom, and a small apartment. Then he designed Via Mizner and Via Parigi, to the delight of Palm Beach denizens. "The idea of taking the air and going shopping in such delightful surroundings was almost unknown at that time in the United States," writes Caroline Seebohm in her Mizner biography, *Boca Rococo*. "Nobody had ever heard of a mall, let alone a theme park."[2]

Within this enchanting setting, Mizner built his pleasure palace. There is a mysterious narrative quality to the entrance sequence of the building,

Above and Opposite: Upon climbing a flight of stone steps, guests enter through this door, glimpsing the dining room lined with fifteenth-century Spanish linen-fold paneling said to have come from the Salamancan apartments of King Ferdinand and Queen Isabella of Spain.

which begins with a pair of massive wooden doors decorated with heavy metal studs and ornate hinges. The cool interior of the foyer is paved with stone and terra-cotta tile and roofed with exposed beams of polychrome wood. A wrought-iron gate offers access from the opposite side and brings in light, while a smaller doorway opens into a narrow stone stair that leads up into the tower. This dark, enclosed ascent delivers the visitor to a bright, barrel-vaulted hallway lined with arched windows that overlook Worth Avenue on one side and Via Mizner on the other. Despite the heavy masonry of the construction, the light-filled gallery seems to float above the street.

Continuing the play of light and shadow, the room directly in front of the entrance is the umbrageous dining room walled with linen-fold paneling taken from the private apartments of King Ferdinand and Isabella of Spain in Salamanca.[3] The floor is paved with terra-cotta tiles made in Mizner's Los Manos factory, where workers created the antique-style hand-crafted materials and furnishings that lent Old World luster to the architect's designs.

Softly tinted light fills the large room at the other end of the loggia—the thirty-five-by-forty-foot living room with walls of parchment-colored stucco, a ceiling of pecky cypress beams, a floor of dark terra-cotta tile surrounding a central oak dance floor, and soaring arched windows of Venetian carved stone, set with stained-glass diamonds in pale tones of violet, yellow, green, and blue. Seebohm paraphrases a contemporaneous description of the decoration of this room: "The Gothic and early Renaissance furniture was upholstered in green, red, and yellow velvet. Richly embroidered tapestries hung from the walls. With pale pink, blue, and green light washing the room through the panes of leaded stained-glass windows, the effect was like a jewel box under water."[4]

The two floors above hold less extravagant rooms—two bedrooms and baths each—while the top floor explodes open to the light, air, and views of town and sea in a mirador. This room, described in *Florida Architecture of Addison Mizner* by his friend and admirer Ida Tarbell, was "a great square place, windows on all four sides, . . . with splendid volumes from every country in the world, studies of the world's architecture, endless portfolios of photographs and etchings and drawings—a collection, too, of those fascinating early maps of the Florida coast, the Gulf and the islands to the South."

Opposite: A massive floor-to-ceiling chimneypiece dominates the central wall of the thirty-five-by-forty-foot living room that spans one end of the villa. Pale stucco walls reflect the light that pours in through tall windows set with diamonds of stained glass. The dark, painted pecky cypress ceilings and terra-cotta tile floors provide warm contrast to the cool color scheme.

"From here," Tarbell continues, one sees best something that Mizner talks much of, and that is the Florida skyline and what it should be—not the forced unnatural imitation of Northern commercial skylines, things endlessly up into the air. There is no call here, along this long Atlantic front, to run up; the natural thing is to run along. "But we want a skyline," they tell you. But look out from Mizner's window and see the true Florida skyline—those red tiled roofs, peaked, variable, at different elevations, and all at such a height that the thing which makes the most beauty against the sky in all Florida, the palm, receives its full value.

NOTES

1. Stephanie Murphy, "Villa Mizner Rich with Memories," *Palm Beach Daily News*, February 2, 2003, p. D1.

2. Caroline Seebohm, *Boca Rococo: How Addison Mizner Invented Florida's Gold Coast* (New York: Clarkson Potter, 2001), p. 190.

3. Ibid., p. 191.

4. Ibid., p. 192.

Below Left: A stairway in Via Mizner is tiled with colorful glazed tiles made in Mizner's Los Manos factory in West Palm Beach, where workers toiled under the architect's specific direction to create handmade building materials that expressed the rich tone and texture of Old World craftsmanship.

Below Right: Mizner Blue was one of the many popular shades of tile manufactured at Los Manos. This fountain in Via Mizner features a number of the shades of blue and green produced at Los Manos.

Eclectic Elegance

A Mid-1920s Spanish-Style House on Snell Isle, St. Petersburg

THE HOME OF HELEN AND PETER WALLACE

"This home is ideally located for viewing the rising sun and especially the full moon in all its gorgeous splendor, rising over the limpid waters of Coffee Pot Bayou and Tampa Bay—o'er which the gentle zephyrs blow." With these words, Samuel V. Schooley described a Mediterranean-revival residence he constructed in the mid-1920s on Snell Isle—a small island of sand and mangrove he helped transform into one of St. Petersburg's most exclusive neighborhoods. C. Perry Snell, the island's primary developer and namesake, built many more elegant residences on these picturesque shores. Helen Wallace grew up in one of Snell's grand houses. She now shares another Snell Isle home nearby (built by Schooley) with her husband, Peter, who also grew up in St. Petersburg. Her husband's brother now lives across the street, and her sister next door—evidence that Schooley's rhapsodic description of the island, though flowery, was far from overblown.

Snell Isle lies just beyond the north shore of St. Petersburg, on the far side of Coffee Pot Bayou and the near side of Tampa Bay. In 1911, Snell purchased the small island, as well as many properties on St. Petersburg's north shore in an area now called Historic Old Northeast. All but a narrow inlet of the Coffee Pot Bayou was filled in by mule teams brought over by Snell from Tampa in order to create high ground for waterfront houses on both sides of the shallow bayou. Snell then began construction of several residences embellished with statuary, tiles, and ornaments he had purchased in Europe, including an imposing Mediterranean-revival home for himself.

Samuel Schooley, a native of Chicago, began purchasing properties near Coffee Pot Bayou in the early 1920s. He commissioned noted architects, including the firm of Kiehnel & Elliott to design homes on speculation on Snell Island and the north shore. Considered by many to be the progenitor of southern Florida's Mediterranean revival style, Richard Kiehnel had already impressed Miami residents with his residential and public buildings, including El Jardin (now the Carrolton School of the Sacred Heart) in Coconut Grove. His design for the Rolyat Hotel (now the Stetson University College of Law), which opened to critical and popular acclaim in St. Petersburg in 1926, was inspired by the idea of a Spanish walled settlement. Its features included an ornate baroque arched entrance, a

Opposite: Few changes have been made since the renowned firm of Kiehnel & Elliott designed this mid-1920s house on Snell Isle. The addition of a copper roof over the entrance arcade and the enclosure of the arched loggia on one corner do not obscure the lively yet dignified asymmetry of the original design.

A Spanish scene composed of hand-painted tile original to the house decorates a wall outside the living room.

Opposite: The original driveway was moved to make room for a walled garden. A long fountain runs along one wall, filling the house with the sound of running water.

Overleaf: The living room's tall windows usher in the breezes that made Snell Isle a popular early-twentieth-century retreat.

massive great hall with polychrome wood ceilings, and two towers, including a reproduction of the Golden Tower of Seville.

Kiehnel's designs for Schooley's homes on Snell Isle borrowed from the same aesthetic, but on a smaller scale and with a less ornate vocabulary. Constructed of steel-reinforced hollow tile, they featured loggias, square towers, and projecting balconies paying equal homage to Spanish and Italian antecedents. "Embodied in the Schooley Homes are liberal features incorporating every desirable and artistic phase of the Mediterranean environment plus the departures of improvement that please individual American tastes and conveniences," boasted Schooley in a brochure illustrating several houses designed by Kiehnel & Elliott. "They are homes that encourage real fascination for abiding in comfort and permanency."

The house the Wallaces purchased five years ago still bears a facade almost identical to that designed by Kiehnel & Elliott seventy-five years before. A triple-bay arcade with a silhouette evocative of the Spanish Baroque marks the entrance to the house. One long wall extends to the right, its three arched windows opening into a large living room. The wing continues, terminating in what was once a loggia with round arches and twisted columns at the far right corner of the house. While the architectural details remain the same, the arches have been glazed to create an enclosed room. The only other changes that alter that facade are the enclosing of a window in the dining room wing to the left of the entrance arcade, and the creation of an iron gallery that unites two individual balconies projecting from second-floor bedrooms.

Within, the house reveals clean, modern lines. Long rectangular rooms are well lit and ventilated by tall doors and casement windows that frame views of the surrounding yard and courtyard. "We wanted an open floor plan with lots of light," said Mrs. Wallace, who with her husband collects contemporary art that coexists congenially with the architectural setting. Two large marble sculptures by New England–based artist Collene Karcher—fragments of a winged figure in the stair hall and a head of Medusa in the living room, offer postmodern Classical references. The attenuated figure of an Asian monk, named *Sake Man* and made by Michigan artist Steven Olszewski, stands on a rough-hewn base next to the living room's grand piano. "I guess we like that tension between contemporary art and antique architecture," Mrs. Wallace observes.

The furnishings and decorative details chosen by the Wallaces reveal an equally eclectic approach to design. Several pairs of chairs in varied styles provide seating in the living room, including upholstered arm chairs purchased at auction from Florida entrepreneur Ed Ball's 1937 Wakulla Springs Lodge and a pair of wrought-bronze chairs purchased by Perry Snell in the 1920s to furnish one of his own island homes. A pair of whimsical bronze lanterns flanking the fireplace came from the Snell Isle house where Mrs. Wallace grew up. The ornately carved Carrera marble fireplace, which the Wallaces purchased at an architectural artifacts store in Tampa, originated from a mansion in New England. A contemporary sculptural coffee table made from salvaged machine parts by Key West–

Opposite: A pair of carved marble Indian columns with dissimilar capitals flanks the opening from the kitchen to a family room added by the Wallaces. The ochre tone of the walls echoes the kitchen's travertine marble as well as the house's exterior stucco.

Above: "Eclectic at best," is how Mrs. Wallace describes the decoration of the living room, which combines a nineteenth-century gilded pier mirror, mid-twentieth-century upholstered chairs, and contemporary art, including this sculpture by Olszewski named Sake Man.

and Asheville-based sculptor Cynthia Wynn stands in the center of the living room.

This blending the antique with the contemporary continues in the informal family room designed by Tallahassee architects Massey-Ledo Studio, which opens off the Wallaces' kitchen. This addition is embellished with a ceiling of rustic exposed beams and a pair of carved marble columns from India. A contemporary painting by Florida artist Rocky Bridges, which incorporates a salvaged sign for garden products, hangs on the ochre wall, overlooking a country French dining table.

Like nearly all the other rooms in the house, this room opens to the outside with several tall French doors. These lead to a series of courtyard spaces that wrap around the house—a long covered loggia, a pool patio, and a walled garden with a low fountain that spans one entire wall. With rectangular tables that can be pushed together to form a large square table in the walled garden or placed end to end in the loggia, the grounds provide ample opportunities for outdoor entertaining. "We bought this house as much for the outside spaces as the inside ones," notes Mrs. Wallace. "We feel like we have another whole house out there."

Casa Mia

A 1925 Ferro-Concrete Spanish Villa in Coral Gables

THE HOME OF DESIRÉE CASKILL
AND LUIS MANUEL PEREZ

Sited on a prominent corner lot, the Coral Gables villa named Casa Mia was intended to attract lasting admiration. Miami's first house constructed entirely from steel-reinforced poured concrete (and North America's third), it was designed in the romantic mélange of Spanish, Moorish, and Italian style that beguiled the state of Florida in the 1920s. With two equally striking facades, one facing Sevilla Avenue, the other Ferdinand (now Alhambra Circle), doors of hammered and wrought bronze, five mosaic fountains, several arcades arrayed on two levels, and a flowering roof terrace, the house commanded attention—then as now.

Current resident Desirée Caskill, a native of Miami, used to gaze at the house daily as a teenager traveling to school at Our Lady of Lourdes Academy. When she drove by as an adult in 1991 and noticed a for-sale sign on the property, she couldn't resist dropping in for a look with her husband, Luis Manuel Perez. "My husband said, 'This is my house,' as soon as he stepped inside," Ms. Caskill recalls. And so Casa Mia, already so named, found its fifth owners.

The house had already enjoyed a colorful history, beginning with its newsworthy construction, which received extensive coverage in a 1926 edition of the *Miami Herald*. The article extolled its novel construction materials and method, noting that "[s]uch a house would be completely fireproof, rainproof, stormproof; impervious alike to time or catastrophe, a lasting monument in a day of restlessness and change." It also highlighted the price of the house—its landscaping, and its contents, "an investment of more than $250,000"—and its eclecticism—"the general impression is of almost monastic Spanish, but closer examination reveals individual touches of Moorish, Indian, Persian, Turkish, and Florentine."

Opposite: An archway mounted with wrought-iron grills creates a mysterious entrance to a stairway leading to the private quarters of the house. Large pots covered with a mosaic pattern of pennies were designed by Franchi de Alfaro, who also designed the living room's tile floor.

Original ceilings of concrete molded to resemble coffered wood and painted with traditional Spanish and Andalusian designs are found throughout the house.

Opposite: *Wrought-bronze gates imported from Barcelona guard the Alhambra Avenue entrance to Casa Mia. The entrance hall also features original polychrome tile door and window surrounds, while the mosaic floor and ceiling decorations were added by the present-day owners.*

Designed by architect F. McM. Sawyer, Casa Mia was unfinished when D. Troy Halls, president of the National Highway Charts Association, purchased it for $75,000. The final structure included eighteen rooms, five of which had coffered concrete ceilings painted to resemble polychrome wood. While the eighteen-foot-high ceiling in the massive living room is ornamented with abstract geometric patterns, the dining room's ceiling bears Spanish crests. The once highly colored smoking room ceiling is now darkened by decades of tobacco smoke, while the master bedroom's delicate floral motifs still reveal their soft, luminous tones.

When Mr. Perez complained that the entrance hall had a plain ceiling, Ms. Caskill commissioned an artist to paint it with a pattern of tropical flora. An interior designer and a preservationist who served on the Coral Gables Historic Preservation Board, Caskill made sure that this ceiling clearly presented itself as a modern addition while complementing the others throughout the house. "I asked the artist to treat the ceiling as a whole canvas rather than breaking up the design into individual coffered squares, like the others," she explains.

Ms. Caskill, who has designed the interiors of Mediterranean and Art Deco houses in Miami and Colonial houses in Central and South America, has a refined understanding of the scale and decoration of such homes. "Some people have a hard time decorating these houses," she comments. "They have such a monumental, serious look—almost monastic." But she likes "everything big"—and grew up in a Cuban-influenced household surrounded by eclectic furnishings.

According to the 1926 *Miami Herald* description of Casa Mia, the original décor was intended to create "a fifteenth century effect . . . [with] furniture transplanted from ancient monasteries and Medici villas and palaces." The dining room included "a Spanish refectory table of dark gumwood where probably many a priest toiled at his labors," "a Spanish credenza, lined with beautiful damask," and "a cabinet used in Ferdinand and Isabella's time." While the master bedroom was decorated in Florentine style, the second floor also included a Persian porch hung with camel bells from Jaffa. Ms. Caskill has perpetuated this tradition of exoticism, mixing a Mexican table and bench with a Hindu altarpiece and Indonesian musical instruments in the dining room. One of the original iron chandeliers, once hanging in the living room, now illuminates the ceiling's age-darkened coffers.

In the living room, various centuries and cultures meet in a successful marriage of styles. Dominant architectural features of the cavernous room include the painted concrete ceiling apparently supported by cast concrete brackets, four Venetian glass mirrored wall sconces built into the walls to cast light upon the ceiling and reflect its glory to passersby, and a sixteen-foot-high plate-glass window that overlooks an exterior fountain. Ms. Caskill added two massive Spanish wrought-iron chandeliers and hired Luciano Franchi de Alfaro to design a mosaic tile floor.

A previous owner had covered many of the house's floors with Cuban tile, but Ms. Caskill felt that the terra cotta was too dark for the house. She and Franchi de Alfaro chose predominately pale colored tiles with warm contrast to brighten the room. He added his signature broken tile details—also favored by Gianni Versace, for whom Franchi de Alfaro had created showroom designs—throughout the pattern. A monumental sofa and pair of chairs with bold black and white upholstery copied from furnishings of Christian Lacroix's Paris showroom add more haute couture detail.

The living room's cast stone fireplace blends Spanish Baroque and Art Deco detail, a large Moroccan lantern injects a Moorish touch, and a Hindu bowery chest adds orientalist exoticism to the décor. Thanks to the huge scale of the eight-hundred-square-foot room, the large furnishings, which also include a baby grand piano and several other upholstered pieces, still give an impression of dignified austerity.

While early accounts describe the effect of Casa Mia to be "as truly fascinating as any tale from the Arabian Nights," its fantastical appeal is not limited to adults. Despite the awe-inspiring proportions and handsome decoration of the house, the family's two young children, Gabriel Alejandro and Claudia Valentina, play boisterously in the space, darting in and out of the house's many terraces and labyrinthine stairways. "Their friends say, 'Oh, you live in a castle!'" Ms. Caskill says laughing, then she agrees. "I guess we do."

Above: A Mexican table and bench lend Spanish Colonial grandeur to the dining room, while Indonesian musical instruments mounted upon the wall lend a note of eclecticism. The iron chandelier originally hung in the living room.

Opposite: A 1926 article describes this "Turkish fountain done in bright tile" near the servant's entrance as well as a "fountain from Tunis with a fountainhead from Constantinople" among the decorative details on the Alhambra Avenue facade.

Previous: An original ceiling of concrete molded to resemble coffered wood soars eighteen feet above the four-hundred-square-foot living room. Wall sconces of painted Venetian glass set high in the walls illuminate the ceiling for the benefit of both inhabitants and passersby who glimpse it through the tall plate-glass window.

The Don Quixote House

A 1926 Coral Gables Casita

THE HOME OF DONNA AND ANTHONY PRISENDORF

In October 1924, *National Builder* magazine published an extensive article entitled "The Story of Coral Gables," describing in detail the "distinctive American suburb that would be a worthy reflection of the architectural enchantment of Old Spain." Picturesque public and commercial buildings were featured, including the Coral Gables Inn, country club, bank, and post office. Phineas Paist, one of the architects who was deeply involved in developing Coral Gables's aesthetic guidelines, contributed a two-page essay about stucco and color, in which he noted that the development's founder, George Merrick, "had the vision and has obtained results by holding control of all architectural and landscape schemes and finally of all the local color of the town."

The result, as noted in this article and still visible today, is a neighborhood of approximately four square miles that is remarkably cohesive in style without ever appearing redundant. "Out of the hundreds of houses at Coral Gables no two are alike," according to this article, published when approximately six hundred homes had already been constructed. "All of the houses bear a strong family resemblance, but there are no twins." However, within a few years, Merrick had decided to inject a few notes of exotic architecture into his mostly Spanish-style city, creating villages that featured whimsical interpretations of other architectural idioms.

The Colonial Village reflected the architecture of the Florida pioneers and the Deep South; the French Normandy and French City Villages interpreted provincial and Versailles-inspired styles; a Chinese Village featured houses with pagoda-form roofs clad in bright yellow, blue, and green tile. While these tiny microcosms added delightfully unexpected intrusions of non-Mediterranean styles, the houses of the Italian Village, inspired by seventeenth-century Italian villas, blend so easily with their Spanish-style

Opposite: The iron gate opens into a loggia that features an arcade supported by twisted columns. At one time open to the garden on the right, the loggia is now an enclosed hallway that connects the house's ground-floor rooms.

Previous: Barrel tiled eaves, rusticated stucco, lancet windows, and a round stair tower add wit, whimsy, and a touch of grandeur to the Don Quixote House, an early Coral Gables bungalow on the edge of the Italian Village.

Right: The arcaded loggia next to the living room was also once open to the garden. Enclosed, it now provides a cozy, light-filled sitting room.

Opposite: The living room's high ceiling, embellished with pecky cypress and carved beams and brackets, and stately cast stone mantel add elegant notes. Ms. Prisendorf selected a bright palette suggestive of tropical greenery and flowers and upholstered chairs and pillows in new and vintage tropical prints.

surroundings that they are hard to distinguish at first sight. A Spanish-style casita named the Don Quixote House stands on the edge of the Italian Village, a reminder of the architectural similarities shared by rustic Spanish and Italian architecture, which led to their easy blending in the Mediterranean revival style.

While many of the homes in Coral Gables were large mansions built for wealthy winter residents, Merrick intended his community to be democratic, providing quality housing at a range of costs. "There is nothing," noted the unattributed author of the *American Builder* article, "that will prevent the building of a more modest home," adding that "there are large areas where cost restrictions are as low as $4,000." However, the strict building guidelines imposed by Merrick ensured that even the most modest home would be aesthetically charming.

In *Coral Gables, Miami Riviera*, a booklet published in 1927, Marjory Stoneman Douglas noted, "The small houses are as carefully worked out as the larger ones, the veranda, arches and doorways as genuinely artistic, with everywhere some touch of decoration, some group of windows, some fascinating line of roof and wall and chimney which indicate the possibility of gracious living within." This description perfectly fits the Don Quixote House, with its wrought-iron garden gate tucked beneath the upswept line of a stuccoed wall, behind which grows a small, arcaded garden. A two-story stair tower rises in the corner of the garden, and, originally, colorful awnings shaded the windows piercing the thick, rusticated stucco walls.

To the right of the gate, a small, square tile is embedded in the pale yellow stucco—its enameled surface decorated with a scene depicting Don Quixote astride Rosinante with lance in hand. Several more such tiles following Don Quixote on his adventure are scattered throughout the house, on the walls of the loggia, the garden, and spiral stair. The iron gate opens into a tiny loggia that faces the walled garden. This loggia, now

enclosed, leads to the stair tower, which is illuminated by tiny arched windows with matching shutters and accented with a rope railing that hangs from metal rings planted in the walls. Don Quixote stands guard on a little tile placed halfway up the stair that leads to the modest bedrooms above.

A window in the interior wall of the enclosed loggia opens into a small dining room, which in turn leads to a diminutive kitchen. Around the corner from the stair tower lies another arcaded loggia facing the garden, this now enclosed as well. Today, it serves as a sitting room—a favorite place for present-day residents Donna and Anthony Prisendorf to relax. "That's a very happy place to read," Ms. Prisendorf notes. "It's nice to have a couple of places where you can settle."

The living room provides another favored spot for reading, gathering with family and friends, or dining for two. "For a little house, the living room is a very nicely proportioned living space," Mrs. Prisendorf points out. "The whole house feels bigger than it is. The rooms are filled with grand gestures that don't take themselves too seriously." For example, the ceiling of the living room is covered with pecky cypress, supported by the same style of carved wood brackets and beams found in Florida's stateliest Spanish-style mansions. But the room's cast stone fireplace is decorated in picturesque style with tiny relief depictions of the *Niña*, the *Pinta*, and the *Santa María*.

Opposite: Lancet windows, a rope railing, and an enameled tile decorated in homage to Don Quixote add further appeal to the delightful spiral staircase.

A diminutive Don Quixote reproduced in a Spanish tile original to the house welcomes guests and residents of the Don Quixote house.

It was this whimsy combined with surprising grandeur that appealed to the Prisendorfs when they bought the house five years ago. Like the state's early seasonal residents who sought a tropical climate and light-hearted architecture in contrast to northeastern homes, the Prisendorfs chose Coral Gables as a winter retreat from their home in Mill River, Massachusetts. Publishers of the *Berkshire Record* newspaper, they also selected Coral Gables in order to be closer to their sons, Justin and Alexis Prisendorf, who publish the *Coral Gables Gazette*.

The couple chose to decorate their Florida bungalow with tropical colors and prints that contrast with their Berkshire home, a turn-of-the-nineteenth-century Massachusetts farmhouse. Prowling New England antiques shops and Massachusetts' famed Brimfield antiques market for furnishings and decorative objects, Ms. Prisendorf found the bamboo chairs that now grace her Florida living room. "You can buy that kind of thing very easily in Massachusetts, because it's not the style up there," she says. She also brought down a bright red poster for the Big Apple Circus, which performs in the Berkshires each year, adding another touch of colorful whimsy to the living room.

When the Prisendorfs come down each winter to relax with family, they enjoy opening all the windows and doors of the bungalow, which is surrounded by tropical gardens. Compared to gardening in New England, where she describes having to "wait and wait and wait until finally a little flower pops up," Ms. Prisendorf revels in the tropical land-scape of her Coral Gables home. "It's so lush, and the tropical plants are all so bold," she says. "When the night-blooming flowers begin to blossom, it's just a fantastic place to be."

Cielito Lindo

A 1928 Mediterranean Revival Mansion in Palm Beach

THE JESSIE WOOLWORTH DONAHUE ESTATE

"Cielito Lindo"—a little bit of heaven . . . a heaven where the walks are not floors of gold and chalcedony, but porcelain tiles, from old Tunis and Barcelona—a heaven, entered into through ancient wrought iron gateways that once barred lovers from rendezvous in the passionate Spanish twilight! And sheltering this "Little Bit of Heaven," a roof of soft rose tiles that had covered and protected an ancient cathedral in a remote part of Cuba—tiles that grew mellow and lustrous as chimes rang for centuries of prayer; toning into mossy edges as generations of señoritas, modest, and señors, more bold, were christened and married and buried.

—MARY FANTON ROBERTS

So rhapsodized style writer Mary Fanton Roberts in her 1928 article in *Arts & Decoration* about the new winter home of five-and-dime heiress Jessie Woolworth Donahue and her husband, James. Describing the 120-plus-room, 45,000-square-foot mansion as "one of the finest Hispanic-American houses in that land of magical dwellings—Palm Beach," she imagines that "'Cielito Lindo' might easily have been the actual handiwork of angels who liked architecture better than harp-playing and who had long dreamed of returning to earth as interior decorators."

In reality, the Hispano-Mauresque pleasure palace was the work of Marion Sims Wyeth, an architect who had studied at Princeton University and the Ecole des Beaux Arts in Paris before working at the distinguished New York firm of Carrère & Hastings. Wyeth formed his own architectural firm, Wyeth & King, and lived in Palm Beach from 1919 until 1982. The first of Palm Beach's architects to be elected to the American Institute of Architects, Wyeth designed more than one hundred Palm Beach houses, the Florida Governor's Mansion, and Shangri La—another little bit of heaven, created in Hawaii for heiress Doris Duke. Along with Addison Mizner, he was one of the best architects working in Palm Beach in the Spanish idiom, mixing and matching a range of Mediterranean influences to create luxuriously romantic estates for the island's elite.

Opposite: The original facade of Cielito Lindo is as rhythmic and romantic as a Spanish dance. Cusped arches of Moorish silhouettes join round Roman arches, columned loggias, and mousharabiya-screened balconies to create a dynamic, delightful effect. Textured white stucco, warm terra-cotta tile, and cast stone decoration successfully unite the disparate elements.

Tiles cover the nine-foot bar in the original barroom, while larger Cuban tiles interspersed with smaller Spanish tiles in shades of blue, yellow, orange, and black pave the floor. Polychrome paneled doors and shutters and a ceiling detailed with eight-pointed stars lends the room a Moorish atmosphere.

Opposite: *The black and white marble tile of the original entrance hall was taken from a ruined cathedral in Santiago. When the current residents purchased the house, a mezzanine floor obscured the tops of the columns and arched, painted ceiling, which has now been revealed and restored to a ceiling height of more than twenty feet.*

Overleaf: *Antique Sri Lankan furniture and mother-of-pearl inlaid mirrors add more exotic detail to the Moorish tower room with views of the ocean and lake. Mrs. Weissman found the original decorative paintwork under layers of obscuring paint and restored the Spanish tile floors to their original luster.*

Much like Mar-A-Lago, the nearby estate belonging to Jessie Woolworth Donahue's sister-in-law, Marjorie Merriweather Post, Cielito Lindo was magnificently sited on a large slice of former jungle spanning from Lake Worth to the Atlantic Ocean. Also like Mar-A-Lago, it boasted a tower that afforded residents and guests panoramic views of the island's sea views and landscapes. In keeping with the Mediterranean mania that swept Palm Beach architecture of the 1920s, the house blends Spanish, Moorish, and Italianate influences, incorporating many antique materials imported from those regions. Despite the fact that the house was nearly bulldozed in the late 1940s to make room for a new subdivision, and was subsequently divided into five individual villas, many of these original materials remain miraculously intact.

What was once the grand entrance to the estate is now the rear facade of the largest of five villas. A three-story-tall tower dominates one end of the building, its bracketed eaves and arched fenestration suggestive of Italianate palazzos. The central segment, however, clearly invokes the Moorish design of Morocco and southern Spain, with its projecting balcony of cusped arches and *mousharabiya*—screens of turned wood traditionally used to hide harems from the eyes of passersby. Entrance-level arcades with stone columns and projecting roofs tiled with antique Cuban barrel tiles add yet more texture and rhythm to the romantic facade. The original front door of cypress, carved and studded with nails, came from Barcelona, and the massive stone wall fountain that faces the original entrance is a replica of one from that city. "It's sweet to live in the right place," reads the inscription in Latin, a translation of a quotation from Homer.

In 1947, Mrs. Donahue, then a sixty-one-year-old widow with grown children, abandoned the sprawling estate to take up winter residence in an apartment in Mizner's Everglades Club on Worth Avenue. Under the direction of architect Bryon F. Simonson of

Opposite: While designer Elsie Sloan Farley created a shell pink and gold Venetian fantasy for Mrs. Donahue's bedroom, Mrs. Weissman and her designer, Jean Caya, designed an elegant French retreat. Nineteenth-century French painted wood panels crown the original French doors and inspired the custom-made bed. A nineteenth-century Aubusson carpet unites the color scheme of delicate dawnlike shades of blue and pink.

Above: Marble columns, Roman arches, and an intricately coffered ceiling detailed the dining room of the original house, which was intended to evoke the Italian Renaissance. In the Donahues' day, according to a contemporaneous account, the room was furnished with "Italian chairs . . . upholstered in old red velvet and the great walnut Renaissance table [that] seats twenty-four happy and enthusiastic guests."

Simonson and Holley, her former home and its service buildings were divided to create five villas of twelve rooms each. The most dramatic change was the demolition of the mansion's sixty-foot-long living room and parallel cloister to make room for Kings Road, a narrow street that now bisects the property.

What was the foyer of the original house became the elegant Italianate living room of 122 Kings Road, the largest of the new villas. Still called Cielito Lindo, this house also retains the original Spanish-style bar, the baronial library detailed with wood paneling removed from the ancestral estate of William Hogarth, the master bedroom suite with its surrounding terrace, and the airy tower room. The current resident, Jody Weissman, worked with Paris–New York–Monte Carlo interior designer Jean Caya to decorate the villa in keeping with the original vision of Old World grandeur formed by the Donahues, their architect, and their interior designer, Elsie Sloan Farley.

Mrs. Weissman added an eighteenth-century Italian marble mantelpiece to the living room and mounted nineteenth-century French panels above the windows in the master bedroom. She removed a mezzanine floor to reveal the stately capitals of the paired columns gracing the former foyer, restored floors of colorful tile, and hired a team of decorative painters to restore the original polychrome details on walls and ceilings

Now the front door of 123 Kings Road, these doors of nail-studded cypress from Barcelona originally graced the facade of Cielito Lindo as the grand entrance to the house.

Opposite: *Many elements of Cielito Lindo's original landscape design, created by landscape architects Lewis & Valentine, remain, including mature palm trees and this charming Neoclassical garden structure overlooking the swimming pool.*

throughout the house. The ongoing restoration has taken four years. Mrs. Weissman has even succeeded in finding some of the original furniture in antiques stores in the area.

Across Kings Road, a street named after the Duke and Duchess of Windsor, who were frequent guests of the Donahues, stands the second half of the main section of the original house. The massive, nail-studded front door of the original house, once facing what is now the rear garden of 122 Kings Road, now opens into the elegant entrance hall of this villa. This stone hall, once part of the massive living room, opens into a soaring Renaissance-style space that once served as the great estate's dining room. Today, it is the living room of Bob Jackson, Carolyn Agresti Jackson, and their young son Robby.

Mr. Jackson marvels at the grandeur of the space—with its soaring marble columns and antique Italian mantelpiece of carved marble, its tall double-hung windows crowned with Roman arches that open to an adjacent outdoors dining terrace. He had dreamed of owning one of Palm Beach's grand mansions ever since he was a child, and finally achieved his dream when he purchased the villa from sisters Kathryn and Ann Hall, who had occupied it since the subdivision occurred. The Jacksons' house also includes a large bedroom suite, most likely one of the larger guest rooms of the original house, two marble-detailed bathrooms, as well as smaller bedrooms, a large dining room, and a kitchen reshaped from other parts of the main dwelling. "Look at these walls—they are thirty-six inches thick," Mr. Jackson points out. "This place is built like a castle."

Three more villas nestle among the old palm trees and fountainlike sprays of bougainvillea that line Kings Road—one formed from the former five-car garage, another from the culinary department, and the final one from the chauffeur's and caretaker's houses. "Individual and distinctive and an outstanding venture in the preservation of building materials that could not be purchased today, each villa bears resemblance to the mother house," wrote a journalist for *Palm Beach Life* in 1949.

The architect who envisioned this creative salvation of a nearly doomed property and the residents who lent their subsequent energies to the ongoing preservation of the Kings Road properties have perpetuated the tradition of excellence that Roberts extolled in her 1928 description of Cielito Lindo and its denizens: "All the people who had anything to do with the creation and developing of the Donahue home seem to have put not only their brain and their strength, but also their imagination and all the gifts of their spirit, into making this the home that Mr. and Mrs. Donahue had dreamed of."

Nuestro Paradiso

A 1928 Palm Beach Mansion

THE ELLIS Z. NUTTING ESTATE

Inspired by a medieval castle in Czechoslovakia, embellished with fanciful sea creatures and gargoyles, and imbued with the imposing grandeur of the Spanish-revival style, Nuestro Paradiso fulfilled all the requirements Mr. and Mrs. Ellis Z. Nutting desired for their Palm Beach home. Magnificently sited on an acre-and-a-half lot reaching from the Atlantic Ocean to Lake Worth, the mansion stretches across the grassy lawn like a recumbent lion, two double-storied sections forming its body and a triple-tiered tower its noble head.

With white stucco-clad walls, varied roof lines encrusted with Cuban barrel tile, and honey-colored quoining, pinnacles, gargoyles, and arched openings, the house is a Spanish fantasy created by Julius Jacobs. The architect combined the ideas brought to the table by the Nuttings, who had recently toured Europe's architectural treasures, with his own experience as a European-born architect and a designer well versed in the Spanish-revival school all the rage in 1928 Palm Beach. The result is a building that marries elegance, eclecticism, and even eccentricity—one section of the house was specifically designed to accommodate a four-ton philharmonic pipe organ that Mr. Nutting, a former sheet music buyer for F. W. Woolworth Company, played.

While the exterior of the house has a linear quality typical of Spanish-revival design, the arched openings of the central bay, and its barrel-vaulted roof, hint at the Baroque curvaceousness that characterizes the interior flow of space. The house is entered through a large Roman-arched doorway flanked by pilasters and surmounted by a balcony. A door of heavy cast iron set with plate glass offers a view into the circular entrance hall and beyond, through a similarly designed doorway, to the patio behind the house. Massive spiral columns support a double-helix stairway that, according to a description of the house written during the Nuttings' residence, was "sculptured on the premises and represents a Spanish hunt of the seventeenth century."

The cast stone stair features friezes depicting hunters on horses in a woodland setting and hounds chasing wild boars. This Old World hunt takes place against a Jazz Age

Opposite: Jacob's facade for Nuestro Paradiso combines rectilinear elements with the curvaceous forms of a central barrel-vault roof and Roman arches to create an asymmetrical appearance that is imposing without being forbidding.

Sea creatures and human-headed lions form a balustrade separating the patio immediately behind the house from terraced gardens that once included a pool, mineral bath, and his and her bathhouses.

Opposite: *The central section of the building is decorated with Churrigueresque details that evoke the decorative flourishes of seventeenth-century Spanish Baroque design. When open, the balcony's windows and doors transform the second floor of the grand stair hall into a loggialike space bringing fresh air and light into the interior.*

Overleaf: *The circular forms of the center stair hall, with its majestic double-helix staircase of cast stone and sunburst-patterned floor of Zenatherium, a cork composite, create a swirling flow of space that sweeps guests into the various entertaining rooms, including a large living room to the left, dining room to the right, and loggialike space on the second floor.*

backdrop created by the floors of Zenatherium—a cork composite popular in the 1920s—laid out in a spiky sunburst pattern of gold, jade, and amethyst points. A barrel-vaulted ceiling spans the second floor of the stair hall, its soaring surface adorned with hand-painted murals depicting signs of the Zodiac. With one side opening through three double doors and two single doors onto a balcony overlooking the grounds and facing the ocean, this room serves as a loggia, enhancing the flow of light and air throughout the first and second floors.

Originally decorated with "a Steinway parlor grand piano, large sofa, several easy chairs, a carved walnut library table, also two smaller tables, oriental rugs on the floor, and several decorative Spanish hangings on the walls," according to the contemporaneous account of the Nuttings' residence (possibly written by one of the Nuttings), the loggia "makes a lovely room for reading and games and for an unobstructed view of the ocean."

This room opened onto a sumptuous master bedroom suite measuring twenty-five by thirty feet, with a five-bay row of casement windows overlooking the sea and a hand-carved bed set upon a platform of waxed oak. The original suite comprised a master bathroom with a vaulted ceiling, a small office, and a dressing room whose contents included an intriguing item described in the early-twentieth-century inventory as "a Battlecreek Vibrator." The upper stories of the house include five guest rooms, the "Echo Organ chamber," several bathrooms, dressing rooms, and a linen closet.

But it is the ground-floor rooms and hidden terraces behind the house that are the most impressive spaces, each equipped and adorned with the unusual details that made Nuestro Paradiso one of the most celebrated entertaining venues in a city renowned for its lavish parties. Upon entering the impressive stair hall, guests would have descended through an arched opening and down four cast-stone steps into the baronial living room. Measuring thirty by fifty feet beneath twenty-foot ceilings, the massive room has a

distinctly Gothic air, with clustered columns, dragon-headed capitals, and clerestory windows with cusped arches.

During the Nuttings' residency, these windows rose above "large woodite grills through which the tones of the swell and great organ [were] heard." These have now been replaced with doors that open into a paneled library and media room, but nearly all the other details of the great hall remain intact, many of them having been restored in an extensive renovation carried out by the early-twenty-first-century owner Bill Elias, of the respected Palm Beach building firm E-mc, Inc. While the Nuttings hosted live concert parties featuring the three-manual Welte Company organ, their guests also benefited from an automatic player equipped with ten rolls that played up to an hour and a half of music broadcast throughout the house with annunciators located in the living room, dining room, and loggia.

In contrast to the living room's long rectangle, the dining room, opening off the north side of the entrance hall through an arched opening decorated with Gothic tracery, is nearly a perfect square. The square form is echoed on the floor of Zenatherium parquet and the deeply coffered ceiling, whose recessed panels are hand-painted with red and grisaille detail and adorned with gilded pendants. Stained-glass windows extend in a triangular bay at the front of the room, ushering in bright light and ocean breezes. A door on the far side of the room opens into an informal dining room whose walls and vaulted ceiling were painted with jungle scenes by a Palm Beach–based WPA artist.

While indoor entertainments were frequent and popular events at the Nuttings' house, it was their pool parties that were the talk of the town in the 1930s. The rear wings of the house, decorated with colorful Spanish tile and a Moorish-style balcony, embraced a patio with a balustrade of cast-stone lions and sea creatures. Beyond this, a terraced lawn landscaped with bougainvillea, hibiscus, croton, sea grape, and gumbo limbo trees surrounded a large saltwater swimming pool and a sulphur bath fed by an artisian well, which offered soothing soaks "similar to what is experienced at one of the sulphur springs resorts." Large his and her bathhouses, now demolished, flanked the pool. A flower garden enclosed by an Australian pine hedge, a rock garden, and small lily pool completed the outdoor offerings of the estate.

Above: Clustered columns complete the Gothic appearance of the dining room's stonework, while the floor of Zenatherium mimics marble parquet. The small, informal dining room viewed through the far doors features jungle-themed murals painted by a WPA artist stationed in Palm Beach.

Nuestro Paradiso's blend of Spanish Baroque Churrigueresque ornamentation, Moorish detail borrowed from Andalusia, and Gothic interior elements is indicative of the exuberant eclecticism practiced by Palm Beach's Spanish-revival architects.

Opposite: *Gothic tracery evocative of ecclesiastical settings decorates the archway leading into the dining room, where inset domes of a deeply coffered ceiling are painted with rich red and grisaille detail.*

Opposite: *The cusped arches of a second-floor balcony overhanging the rear patio reveal the exotic Moorish influence that characterized the architecture of southern Spain and appealed to Florida's early-nineteenth-century architects and their clients.*

Above: *While the imposing facade of Nuestro Paradiso is welcoming only to those who have been invited, the exterior, which faces a private playground, offers an open and engaging progression of spaces.*

"[T]he ideal Palm Beach home of the 1920s was a place of private retreat, as well as social gathering," conclude the authors of a 1991 Landmarks Preservation Commission report describing Nuestro Paradiso. "This house was both, in that the . . . decoration and arrangement of space could be . . . impressive to the visitor, yet very aloof and formal to the uninvited. . . . These elements are important to the understanding of the social ideals in the history of Palm Beach."

Timeless Style

A 1932 Spanish-Style House in St. Petersburg

THE HOME OF JOE AND ROBIN REED

The Old Northeast neighborhood of St. Petersburg is one of Florida's lesser-known yet most intact historic residential districts. Placed on the National Register of Historic Places in 2003, the subdivision stretches from downtown St. Petersburg to the shores of Tampa Bay and Coffee Pot Bayou, its brick-paved streets lined with houses in a range of revival styles. Spacious Mediterranean, Tudor, and Colonial revival houses share shaded sidewalks with modest Arts and Craft bungalows, Mission-style casitas, and vernacular Florida cottages. Old plantings of massive oaks and banyon trees, jacarandas, palms, and magnolias serve as a unifying force, modulating the shifts in scale and ornamentation from street to street.

Established in 1911, when C. Perry Snell (also the developer of nearby Snell Isle) and J. C. Hamlett began to pursue their vision of creating a luxurious St. Petersburg waterfront neighborhood, what became Historic Old Northeast rode the crest of the Florida land boom, and managed to stay afloat when it ended. Due to its proximity to the waterfront (and a waterfront park system created in the early twentieth century) and to commercial areas downtown, the neighborhood continued to attract homeowners throughout the 1930s and beyond. These included Helen Rose Pace, the owner of an exclusive dress shop, and her husband, Virgil, who demonstrated, according to a March 21, 1932, article in the *St. Petersburg Times*, "further evidence of their confidence in the future of St. Petersburg" by awarding a contract for the construction of a $20,000 home in the heart of the neighborhood.

Described in the same article as "a two-story Spanish type of reinforced hollow tile construction, faced with stucco and trimmed with stone with wrought iron balconies and grilles embellishing the design," the house was the last of several the couple constructed in St. Petersburg. It replaced their previous home, which still stands nearby. While these houses share several features, including elaborately tiled bathrooms, the ultimate Pace home also includes a baronial living room, whose soaring ceiling is said to have been inspired by the Great Hall of Kiehnel & Elliott's Rolyat Hotel, which opened in St. Petersburg in 1926.

Opposite: A cast stone door surround inspired by Spanish Baroque architecture lends an elegant air to the otherwise restrained stucco facade of this house designed in 1932 by St. Petersburg–based architect Elliott Hadley.

Illuminated by what today is termed a Palladian window, crowned with a cathedral ceiling, and enclosed by walls "finished in three shades of transparent water colors," a contemporaneous description of the living room might easily be mistaken for that of a modern-day luxury dwelling. At the time, it was the final word in Mediterranean-style elegance, invoking the feudal grandeur of Spain with its heavy trusses of antiqued wood stenciled in "Spanish colors" and its balcony and stairway embellished with ornamental wrought-iron railings. Mrs. Pace, who was later divorced and remarried to William Lawler, lived in the house until her death in 1982. Affectionately known as St. Petersburg's Queen of Fashion, Mrs. Lawler lived in stylish elegance in her Historic Old Northeast home.

When the city began to suffer from urban blight in the mid-to-late twentieth century, Mrs. Lawler supported numerous community betterment projects and told an interviewer from *St. Petersburg* magazine in 1963 that she was "quite taken [with St. Petersburg]—enraptured—very much in love." Joe and Robin Reed, who retired to St. Petersburg from New Jersey in 1999, also fell in love with St. Petersburg, and Mrs. Lawler's home, making an offer on it almost as soon as they saw it. "If you love old houses, how could you resist?" asks Mrs. Reed. "We were only the third owners. All the original materials were here—just the kitchen had been changed."

The original materials that appealed to the Reeds included not only the living room's stenciled ceiling beams and iron balustrade, but also original wrought-iron light fixtures, more stenciled beams in the sunken dining room, and a pair of iron gates that opened into the room. Mrs. Reed also loved the master bathroom on the second floor, which also includes four bedrooms and another tiled bath. The master bath marries Art Deco geometry with Spanish Baroque details, with walls of gleaming aqua and black tiles, arches, and twisted columns. Fortunately, the bathroom has survived virtually unchanged since its construction. Even the original fixtures are still in place, including a yellow ceramic pedestal sink and bathtub and a chromium-plated Swedish shower with multiple jets, which provided the ultimate in spa-style bathing, then as now.

Above and Opposite: Hand-applied plaster, stenciled trusses, and wrought-iron light fixtures and stair railings add texture and romantic detail to the large two-story living room, reputedly inspired by the Great Hall at the 1926 Rolyat Hotel.

When the Reeds interviewed architects to remodel and enlarge the kitchen and garage areas of the house, they quickly dismissed one who suggested modernizing the master bath. However, they did decide to update the kitchen and maid's room, creating a wall of French doors and transom windows that open up to the pool and terrace beyond. They hired local craftsmen to make the doors and cabinetry and imported handmade, hand-painted tile from Portugal to decorate the walls after visiting a tile factory in Sintra, outside Lisbon.

The view the French doors frame is the Reeds' creation—a walled garden with a tiled pool terrace that replaces a driveway that had added little charm to the rear elevation of the house. Working with an expert contractor, they also embellished the once plain side of the house with wrought-iron brackets, grilles, and barrel tiled eyebrows that match details found elsewhere in the house. These changes increase the ease of flow between the house's indoor and outdoor spaces, allowing the Reeds to spend much of their time outside.

Above: The Reeds made several trips to Portugal to select the hand-made, hand-painted tiles that grace their remodeled kitchen and landscaped garden beyond the French doors.

Opposite: Wrought-iron gates separate the entrance hall from the original dining room, which is sunk two steps below the main level of the house.

Each resident since Mrs. Pace has introduced a new element to the house without undermining its original character or appearance. The second owner added Italianate details within and without, including a stone balustrade on the exterior, tall cypress trees along the front, and a mural depicting the Italian countryside in the breakfast room. The Reeds restored a mural in the bar room, commissioned by the original residents, which depicts Prohibition-era Floridians capering in bars and beneath palm trees and suggests that parties there were not dry affairs. By improving the landscaping of the house and increasing access to the surrounding yard, the Reeds have found that they can live in the house in true old-Florida style. "This house is really comfortable without air-conditioning five or six months out of the year," Mr. Reed remarks. "We sleep with the windows open and eat breakfast outside," his wife adds. "It's perfect."

Opposite: The house's first resident, who owned a prominent dress shop, commissioned a master bathroom in the height of 1930s style, including Spanish architectural details, colorful tile, and modern, luxurious fixtures.

Spanish Modern

A 1934 Art Deco/Spanish-Style House in Miami Beach

THE HOME OF HENRY AND MARGARITA COURTNEY

The Mediterranean revival was established as the first architectural style of choice for Miami Beach as soon as developer Carl Fisher had completed the wood bridge connecting the spit of land then known as Ocean Beach to the Miami mainland. Merging his resources with those of John Collins, who owned most of the island property and had constructed the first half of the bridge, Fisher began dredging sand from the bottom of Biscayne Bay and depositing it on the island in 1913. By 1915, the island was christened Miami Beach—and by 1920, the Flamingo Hotel, with its eleven-story tower crowned with a multicolored dome—opened for business.

By the mid-1920s, upscale tourists who traveled to Florida via Henry Flagler's railroad or by car on the recently extended Dixie Highway basked in the sun at Miami Beach's Roman Pools, a pleasure grounds complete with Mediterranean-style bathing pavilions, a domed tower, and eye-catching windmill. Across the street, the Romney Plaza Hotel, designed by Biltmore Hotel architects Schultz & Weaver, exemplified the restrained elegance of the Mediterranean revival style, with long arcades paralleling the street fronts and an imposing tower rising at one corner.

But Miami Beach's—and Florida's—newfound prosperity was fragile, and it took little more than a series of misfortunes to halt the resort city's construction. Sensational exposés deploring the shady practices of Florida real estate salesmen, a railroad embargo combined with a maritime accident blocking Miami Harbor, and a violent hurricane brought the land boom to an end in 1926. Land values collapsed and new building came to a standstill. The ascendance of the Mediterranean revival style of architecture in Miami Beach—with its classical forms hinting at Old World permanence—halted as well.

When prosperity returned to Miami Beach in the middle of the next decade, it ushered in a new style of architecture that looked forward, with sleek geometric forms and modern materials including steel-reinforced concrete, plate glass, and neon, rather than back. "The more than 500 Art Deco buildings built almost entirely during the 1930s, addressed that epoch's rapture with travel (the car, the ocean liner, the locomotive), industrialism, Hollywood glamour, and the exoticism of Latin culture," writes architectural historian Laura Cerwinske.[1]

Opposite: The Courtneys' house turns a decidedly Art Deco facade to the street with a long, low wall and wrought-iron gate with a rhythmic pattern of scrolls. The use of terra cotta, however, reinforces the Spanish appearance of the wall.

Overleaf: The front gates open into a courtyard that is purely Spanish in style, with four arcaded walls surrounding a patio floored with Cuban tile and filled with a quatrefoil stone fountain.

While these aggressively modern new buildings sprang up along South Beach and the shopping mecca of Lincoln Road, wealthy homeowners began building houses that married the rhythmic geometry of the Art Deco style with the gracious elegance of the Mediterranean revival style in residential areas. The home of Henry and Margarita Courtney, located on the Indian Creek Waterway in the Pine Tree/La Gorce neighborhood exemplifies the timeless stylishness of these dwellings.

Approached from a tree-shaded boulevard that parallels the waterway and ocean beyond, the house presents a formidable walled facade that communicates to passersby the cloistered privacy of the interior spaces. The pale ochre stucco surface of the wall, the scalloped edge of terra-cotta barrel tiles, and the iron-gated entranceway all suggest the Spanish influence. But the sharp-edged geometry of the walled facade and the rhythmic scrollwork of the gate's wrought iron create a distinctly Art Deco impression.

Within the gate, the house presents a courtyard that is entirely Old World Spanish in its mood, with a four-sided arcade enclosing a tile-floored patio. Cast stone columns support three round arches on each side of the patio, which features a cast stone fountain in its center. "When we came inside the house and I saw the courtyard, I said, 'How beautiful!'" recalls Mrs. Courtney, who purchased the house eight years ago with her husband, Henry. Mrs. Courtney, who grew up in Spanish Colonial surroundings in Puerto Rico, "loved the idea of the courtyard, the way every room looks outside, into the courtyard, or across the water on the other side."

The house was constructed in 1934, designed by architect Robert E. Collins, who was one of Miami Beach's preeminent architects of the 1930s. While Collins designed many residences for upscale clients, he is best known for his theater designs, including the Lincoln and Cameo Theatres. His design for the house now owned by the Courtneys reveals his talent for creating dramatic sequences of spaces and blending decorative elements from classical and modern vocabularies.

By the time the Courtneys bought the house, their four children had already grown up and moved on. Mrs. Courtney, who owns a shop named Margaux that offers eclectic, exotic home furnishings and interior design services, enjoyed the opportunity to decorate the house "as a grown-up house." Drawing upon their travels to the Mediterranean (a trip to Italy inspired the pale ochre shade of the exterior, which reminds Mrs. Courtney of the colors of Florence) and India, the couple filled the spacious courtyard and entertaining rooms with furniture and artwork that reflect a worldly sophistication.

Dark-finished wood benches inset with colorful tiles offer seating in the shaded arcades around the courtyard. Although reminiscent of Spanish Colonial furniture in Mexico, they actually came from India. A screened doorway with a cusped horseshoe arch leans against one wall in the dining room, lending another touch of Indian exotica to the décor. A carved wood door from India serves as a coffee table in the living room, its large scale complementing the grand proportions of the room.

Opposite: Reproduction Art Nouveau tapestries hang in the stair hall, where a spiral staircase with stone steps and Art Deco-style ironwork creates a glamorous mood.

Left: Ms. Courtney continues the theme of exotic eclecticism in the dining room, where she mounted an Indian screened door panel along one wall.

The room's tall ceiling is crisscrossed with wooden beams. One wall of windows overlooks the courtyard, and another, a paved pool terrace on the opposite side of the house, which overlooks the Indian Creek Waterway. Designed for optimal cross-ventilation, the room basks in bright sunlight. In order to create a soothing visual effect, Mrs. Courtney chose a greenish taupe for the room's walls and ceiling, with a contrasting panel of terra-cotta-colored paint for the projecting chimneypiece.

The room flows easily through arched doorways into the dining room on one side and on the other side to a stair hall accented with a graceful spiral staircase of cast stone and iron. Like the rest of the house, this architectural element (with its antique-looking stone steps and jazzy iron railing) marries Old World sophistication and modern sensibilities. "This is a very elegant house, even without any furniture," says Mrs. Courtney. "This is a house for the soul."

NOTE

1. Laura Cerwinske, *South Beach Style* (New York: Abrams, 2002), p. 35.

House of Stone

A 1936 Coral Rock Cottage in Coral Gables

THE HOME OF JOSÉ GELABERT–NAVIA
AND MEL REA MAGUIRE

The Venetian Pool forms the heart of Coral Gables, the planned city George Merrick masterminded with both practical and romantic intent in the early 1920s. Beginning with a 160-acre truck farm outside Miami, Merrick acquired several thousand acres more and began developing it as "The suburb where castles in Spain are made real!"[1] He and his team of architects, landscape architects, and engineers laid out a planned city with wide boulevards and regular streets, ornamental gateways, and large plazas, a commercial district, a golf course, and the Venetian Pool. The latter was an abandoned quarry decked out with Venetian-style lanterns mounted on painted posts, pavilions and dressing rooms of coral stone clad with stucco, and roofs of antique terra-cotta barrel tiles imported from Cuba.

The 1926 bust of the Florida land boom undermined the fulfillment of Merrick's vision of an upscale town filled with elegant coral gabled mansions (so named for the color of the preferred red tile roofs). But despite the many challenges Coral Gables encountered over several decades, Merrick's underlying plan and overarching aesthetics still provided a strong foundation. Thanks to a rigorous preservation movement active today, the present-day Gables is a remarkably coherent and stylistically unified neighborhood that resembles in many ways the "city like an artist's dream set in a great open garden," that Merrick had envisioned.[2]

Architect Dean Parmelee came from New York in 1927 to work as an architect in Miami. Arriving upon the heels of the 1926 bust, the architect quipped, "It was cheaper to starve in Miami than in New York." Post-bust Miami proved surprisingly fertile ground for the architect, who designed many homes in eclectic styles, as well as several banks, churches, and a hotel. But according to contemporary architect and architectural historian José Gelabert-Navia, his most remarkable achievement is the Coral Gables cottage he built across Toledo Street from the Venetian Pool—a house where Parmelee lived for four years, and where Mr. Gelabert-Navia now resides with his wife, Mel Rea Maguire.

Opposite: The rosy roofline of terra-cotta barrel tiles makes clear the inspiration of the name Coral Gables, which the city's founder, Merrick, dubbed his visionary planned development. Indigenous coral stone was another of the building materials Merrick favored.

A tiny gargoyle (not original to the house) guards a garden entrance, adding more charm to the picturesque cottage.

Opposite: Wood doors, window surrounds, and gates painted bright red provide vivid contrast to the gray-brown walls of the cottage built in 1936 from coral stone, or oolithic limestone.

Parmelee built the house in 1936, using oolithic limestone, or coral stone, left over from the Venetian Pool and quarried from his own land, as well as cypress, which he claimed "could be readily obtained in large beams." Though modest in size, the house appears to ramble across its corner lot, with low-pitched roofs of varying height covered in barrel tile that contrasts warmly with the rough brown-gray stone walls. Red shingle tiles embedded randomly among the irregular blocks of coral stone add more color and interest to the walls, and doors and window surrounds painted bright red contribute highlights. Surrounded by heavy tropical foliage and two large and ancient bouganvilleas, the cottage and its walled garden present a remarkably picturesque tableau.

"The wall and the overgrown landscaping made the house appear impenetrable," recalls Mr. Gelabert-Navia, who used to bring students from Miami's School of Architecture to the corner to make freehand drawings of the Venetian Pool and the cottage across the street long before he owned it. "Imagining the owners as being eccentric, I never ventured inside." Many years later, when the architect and his attorney wife were searching for a home, they discovered that the house was on the market. A tour of the interior immediately sparked Mr. Gelabert-Navia's interest.

The house is built around a central courtyard that Parmelee described as "an out-of-door living room 20 by 25 feet." Walled on four sides, this space was open to the sky, with covered hallways on either side that led to bedrooms. The main living room opens onto this courtyard. With walls of light-painted cypress boards and massive dark cypress beams supporting a balcony and vaulted roof, it also creates the impression of a large and soaring space. "High ceilings afford coolness as well as spiritual uplift," Parmelee noted of the design.

While Mr. Gelabert-Navia and Ms. Rea Maguire admired the courtyard plan of the house, they decided to build a roof over the courtyard to create another large living space that could be used year-round. Mr. Gelabert-Navia designed a pitched, open-beamed ceiling poised above a row of clerestory windows in order to maintain the open feeling and natural light of the original courtyard. Made of wide cypress boards painted pale green, the ceiling floats above the room's stone walls and slate floor, creating an airy central space that contrasts with the earthier, more enclosed rooms surrounding it.

The windows of this covered
walkway paralleling the
enclosed courtyard were
originally unglazed, turned-
wood spindles forming
the only division between
interior and exterior space.

Overleaf: The houses'
present-day resident,
architect Gelabert-Navia,
enclosed the central courtyard to create a second large
living room. By using
clerestory windows and a
pale, vaulted roof, he
maintained the airy
atmosphere of the space
that was originally open
to the sky.

Finding the original bedrooms too small for daily use, the current residents also added a master bedroom suite. In keeping with the textures of the rest of the house, the floors of the bedroom addition are tile and the walls are constructed of wide cypress boards with intersecting beams painted a darker shade. The pitched ceiling echoes the rooflines found elsewhere in the house, but careful consideration was taken to ensure that this addition, though sympathetic to the 1936 structure, did not masquerade as part of the original house. The residents also added a breakfast room that looks out into the walled tropical garden and built a roof terrace overlooking the Venetian Pool.

"We have the only house that looks into the pool," Ms. Rea Maguire notes, adding that she and her husband often enjoy a glass of wine together in their unusual perch. When sitting on the terrace, or in the courtyard where Parmelee had sat sixty-five years before, Mr. Gelabert-Navia marvels at the coincidental similarities linking himself and his predecessor. "I wondered how this house could have two owners that were both architects, and whose fathers were architects as well, . . . who married women whom they met on blind dates, both of whom were attorneys. Perhaps it was fate; perhaps it is just the magic of the house."

Above: A master bedroom addition echoes the proportions, shapes, and materials of the original house without imitating them.

Opposite: The original living room has a soaring ceiling and balcony that once housed Parmelee's office.

Overleaf: A roof terrace overlooking the Venetian Pool is a favorite spot for Mr. Gelabert-Navia and Ms. Rea Maguire.

NOTES

1. George E. Merrick, "The Realization of an Ideal," *Miami Daily Metropolitan*, November 14, 1921, n.p.

2. Ibid., p. 2.

El Cortijo

A 1937 Country Spanish-Style House in Winter Park

THE HOME OF JEANNIE AND CHARLIE HARRIS

While many of the renowned creators of Florida's Spanish style drew inspiration from the urban architecture of old Spain or grand palaces including the Alhambra, Florida architect James Gamble Rogers II—known as Gamble Rogers—was intrigued by *cortijos*. In contrast to the ecclesiastical grandeur and imposing proportions that other Spanish-revival architects emulated, these rustic country farmhouses had a tactile quality contributed by rough, hand-hewn materials and informal massing. Often built over a period of a century or more, these Spanish farmhouses had often been added onto over the years as extended families grew. Their interior spaces, courtyards, arcades, and balconies seemed built not to impress, but to accommodate, and to foster a harmonious relationship between the residents and their natural surroundings.

An architect with a passion for romantic revival styles (he also excelled in Tudor, Colonial, and French Provincial revival styles), Rogers favored a succession of intimately scaled rooms and engaging transitional spaces that charmed and embraced residents and their guests. "When I came in the front door and looked down the hallway with the arches, I thought, this is so romantic," recalls Jeannie Harris of her first encounter with the 1937 Gamble Rogers house she and her husband purchased six years ago. "We immediately liked the scale of the house, as opposed to the new homes being built with such oversized proportions. When you walk in here, you have the feeling of an old Mediterranean house with just the right dimensions."

While Mrs. Harris was searching for a house in a more formal Mediterranean revival style blending Italianate and Spanish elements, she and her husband fell beneath the spell of the house Rogers designed for the son of Rollins College's beloved president, Hamilton Holt. Much like the *cortijos* that inspired the architect, the Holt house had been enlarged several times, with a bedroom wing connected to the original house by an engaged tower, a large family room created by enclosing a terrace, a modern kitchen and dining room, a screened porch, and a separate garage designed to look like a guest house from the rear.

The first major addition was carried out by Rogers in 1941. His son Jack Rogers (an architect with offices in Winter Park today) designed the second addition, completed

Opposite: The rear, lakeside elevation of the house (shown here) is much more Italianate in style than the romantic Spanish country style street-front facade.

A one-and-a-half story tower graces the street-front facade, adding a picturesque element and uniting two wings of disparate height. Earthy materials including hand-made terra-cotta barrel tiles add more rustic charm.

Opposite: *The original house's living room, this chamber accommodated frequent entertainments during which musicians performed from the balcony opening off the second-floor bedrooms.*

Overleaf: *This arcade once opened to an outdoor terrace, transformed into a baronial drawing room in 1972. Designed by the original architect's son, Jack Rogers, the room reflects Gamble Rogers's influence in scale and ornamentation, with the hand-hewn ceiling beams and built-in wood bookshelves flanking the mantel.*

in 1972. As a result, the enlarged dwelling still manifests the unity of scale and style intended by the original architect. One major stylistic change that occurred during the first remodeling, however, was the addition of Italianate elements to the rear terrace, including a stone balustrade. This lakeside facade satisfied Mrs. Harris's desire for Mediterranean-style grandeur, while the rustic Spanish touches, including the cantilevered balcony on the street-side facade and the rough-set mortar of the exterior walls, increased her appreciation for the Spanish Provincial style.

The Harrises restored the house's interior to a close approximation of its original appearance, removing wallpaper and paneling, replastering walls with hand-applied, whitewashed plaster, staining interior woodwork dark brown, and rewiring hand-wrought iron light fixtures. The resulting décor complemented Mrs. Harris's traditional tastes and her husband's more modern aesthetic. The couple's eclectic furniture and decorative objects, including Art Deco–style club chairs and Chinese ceramics, fill the rooms without detracting attention from the handsome architectural details.

Gamble Rogers was known for his attention to detail. At Casa Feliz, the Spanish-style residence he created in Winter Park for Robert Barbour, he invented a special whitewash to soften the glow of brick salvaged from the old Orlando Armory. Barrel roof tiles handmade in Barcelona by workers who formed them over their thighs covered the low-pitched roof, while a stone arch was deliberately chipped around the edges to create an illusion of antiquity.

Although by comparison George Holt's house was modest in size, it nonetheless abounded in detail, including scenic hand-painted tiles salvaged from Spain's Hotel Seville set into the stucco walls at intervals. An interior balcony with turned spindles and columns creates an unexpected approach to the second-store bedrooms while serving double duty as a minstrel's gallery above the original living room. A former occupant who lived in the house for twenty years described a dinner party at which the men's choir from Rollins College performed from this balcony.

JAMALI
THE ROSE

Opposite: Varied ceiling heights and pitch, as well as turned spindles and columns, add interest to this transitional space that overlooks the original living room and connects a pair of original bedrooms to the spiral staircase.

Right: Painted tile scenes salvaged from Spain's Hotel Seville are embedded in the house's thick plaster walls. Pegged, hand-hewn wood provides rustic frames for the three scenes located in various parts of the house.

However, family dinners were usually held outside, on the lakeside courtyard (enclosed in 1972 to create the family room). Cool breezes ruffled starched linens, and servants trod to and from the tiny kitchen. Today, the Harrises enjoy most meals on a screened porch they designed, copying a Moorish arch found elsewhere in the house for the exterior walls and paving it with Turkish tile. But they cook their meals without the help of servants in a spacious modern kitchen added in 1972.

Like previous residents, Mrs. Harris has left her imprint upon the landscaping of the house, creating a sunken forecourt embellished with a quatrefoil fountain that reiterates the form of the tower's clerestory windows. She and Mr. Harris chose a pale ochre tone for the exterior of the house, which had been painted pastel green when they purchased it. In order to re-create the antique appearance of the terra-cotta barrel tiled roof, which was badly in need of replacement, they imported handmade tiles from France that mimicked the irregular rosy tones of the originals.

"We wanted to bring the house back, inside and out, to the original Spanish style," explains Mrs. Harris. Celebrating both rustic simplicity and sophisticated ornamental detail, the Harrises' restoration, as well as the additions of previous owners, has kept the spirit of the original house alive. A tribute to the enduring appeal of Gamble's beloved country Spanish style, the house also testifies, along with many of the architect's other surviving Winter Park designs, to his enduring contribution to the city's celebrated aesthetic charms.

Ranch Redux

A Remodeled Ranch House in Miami

THE HOME OF JOHN AGUIRRECHU-CLARK

When John Aguirrechu-Clark purchased a home on Granada Boulevard, in the heart of Coral Gables in Miami, he bought a simple ranch-style house with little architectural distinction. Constructed in 1949, the low-slung house incorporated several interconnected living spaces. These included a living room and dining room with flat ceilings and long, uninterrupted walls that accommodated his growing collection of paintings by Cuban-born, New York–based artist Manuel Pardo. "When I bought the house, everything was on one level, and all the ceilings were low," Dr. Aguirrechu-Clark recalls. The paintings, with their earthy colors, modulated tones, and swelling volumes, lent drama to the space.

In 1996, a fire destroyed a large portion of the house. Fortunately, most of the paintings were spared, and these provided a starting point for rebuilding the house under the guidance of Alan Tibaldeo, a childhood friend of Dr. Aguirrechu-Clark. When he hired Tibaldeo, Dr. Aguirrechu-Clark gave him very little direction. "I knew he was very good with proportions, and that he knew my art collection," he explains. "I told him, 'I need three bedrooms, three bathrooms. Do whatever you want.'"

"The paintings were a preestablished collection," says Tibaldeo. "So they became an intrinsic part of the project. Manuel's aesthetic is comparable to what I like to do." One of Pardo's paintings hangs on a wall that divides the entrance hall from the main body of the house. Two figures are densely packed into the canvas, their flattened forms overlapping, united by the red crescent shape of a hand-held fan. "I love layering," Alan explains, pointing out how walls in varying shades of paint overlap one another in the entrance hall, then open up to create a narrow rectangle through which a succession of rooms can be viewed.

"I also love to frame things," the architect explains. This passion shows up again and again in the house, whether in a slice of clerestory window that outlines an oblong of sky in the high-ceilinged entrance tower or the asymmetrical mantel of curved plaster that forms an architectonic setting for a small fireplace in the living room. In the entertaining area of the house, each room serves not only as a space within itself, but also as a frame for the room next door or the external view beyond.

Opposite: When Miami-based architect Tibaldeo redesigned Dr. Aguirrechu-Clark's 1950s ranch house, he added a compressed tower and surfaced the exterior in painted stucco-details that gave the exterior a Spanish-style appearance.

Tibaldeo broke up the flat, linear quality of the ranch house's original rooms by lifting the ceiling of the living room to parallel the slope of the roof truss and adding an asymmetrical curved fireplace surround.

Opposite: *A vaulted roof, clerestory window, and large Moorish lantern all lend the entrance tower's interior a Spanish flavor. However, a wall that appears to float in space and a spare rectangular doorway that frames the open flow of rooms beyond create a modernist impression.*

In the living room, Tibaldeo created a slanting ceiling that follows the slope of the roof. Preexisting ductwork creates a horizontal line along one wall. The architect created another contour by framing the door opening to the dining room with a deep lip of plaster upon which stands a collection of Moroccan metal lamps. "Morocco was my inspiration for some of the colors in the house," says Dr. Aguirrechu-Clark, whose love of sun-warmed tones of terra cotta and raw umber also reflects influences from his childhood in Santo Domingo.

While Tibaldeo used the opportunity of redesigning the ranch house to inject an element of the edgy modernism he associates with twentieth-century Miami, he also drew upon his client's interest in Latino art and Spanish-style architecture. This influence is most clearly revealed in the entrance hall, which the architect transformed into a tower, lending drama to the low profile of the house. The enclosed loggia that parallels the

Like the loggias popular in Spanish-style houses of the early twentieth century, this long hallway was originally designed to be open to the air. It was later enclosed with plate glass doors that still allow natural light to flow into the space.

*The master bedroom
features a suite of furniture
designed by modernist
master Eliel Saarinen.
The architect designed a
corridor of doors that
alternately reveal and
conceal closets, dressing
rooms, and the master bath.*

bedroom wing adds another reference to Spanish-style residential design. With floors of stained and polished cement and a wall of terra-cotta-colored pillars interspersed with tall glass doors that open onto a terrace, the hallway, though enclosed, offers the atmosphere of a sun-drenched loggia.

Trained in modernism, the architect notes that he "tends not to decorate things." Instead, he claims an interest in proportions, and the relations of shapes and volumes to one another. These proclivities helped transform Dr. Aguirrechu-Clark's simple ranch house into a dynamic interior space whose volumes and vistas provide an engaging setting not only for the resident's art collection, but also for his growing collection of Art Deco and classic modern furniture.

The living room's angles and curves complement the streamlined shapes of French Art Deco arm chairs, sofa, and a glass and wood coffee table of the same period. Another small sitting room that occupies a crossroads junction of spaces in the center of the house commands attention with a zebra-skin rug and a pair of Harry Bertoia diamond chairs. A long room at the rear of the house—formerly a screened Florida room—is decorated in understated 1950s elegance with long, straight falls of curtains, an undulating chaise longue, and a long, low sofa.

Modern minimalism finds full expression in the master bedroom—a plain white chamber with a sloping ceiling and a hall of polished birch doors that hide closets and dressing rooms. A rare suite of furniture designed by Eliel Saarinen fills the room, its serenely spare geometry punctuated by the rhythmic placement of curved wood and metal drawer pulls. "I use this room only for sleeping," says Dr. Aguirrechu-Clark, "so I wanted it to be very simple and restful."

While fulfilling the resident's request, Tibaldeo satisfied his own sense of creativity by designing a complex arrangement of doors leading from the bedroom, past a dressing and closet area, to the master bath. "I studied all the variations of the door openings in a maquette," he recalls, demonstrating how doors can be shut to separate the hallway from the bedroom and the bath, opened to create an uninterrupted corridor, or partially closed to create two separate dressing areas. "I love working things to the max," the architect concludes.

Pale terra-cotta-colored stucco and deep overhanging cornices contribute traditional Spanish-style elements to the otherwise modern poolside facade of the house.

Hispano-Modern

A 2000 Modernist Mediterranean Revival House in Coconut Grove

A HOME DESIGNED BY SUZANNE MARTINSON

Jay and Devon Cross came to Miami-based architect Suzanne Martinson with an interesting problem. Fans of modernist architecture, they had just purchased a lot in a new subdivision in Coconut Grove that required homeowners to construct their houses in the Mediterranean revival style. Martinson, a modernist architect who has lived in Miami since she was five, surrounded by the city's blend of Mediterranean revival and early modernist architecture and its tropical landscape, was the perfect candidate for the job.

"I have a great affinity for the Miami landscape and the tropical environment," says Martinson. "I'm intrigued with the idea that modernism can lend itself to our tropical environment. The ideas of opening up walls for ventilation, using shade protection, bringing the outdoors in, playing with the line that defines indoor-outdoor space—these all lend themselves to modernist interpretations." Interestingly, these are the same issues that intrigued Addison Mizner and other early-twentieth-century proponents of the Spanish style of architecture, who used its vocabulary of loggias, courtyards, and overhanging cornices in response to the same landscape and climate.

However, with the exception of deep, shade-providing cornices, Martinson chose not to exploit these typical Spanish-style elements in the house she designed for the Crosses. "I try to avoid them," she says. "I want a different type of experience." Instead, she created a minimalist, planar facade that draws upon classical Mediterranean tripartite proportions, with a clearly defined base (which dark green climbing vines help to define), a piano nobile of white-painted stucco, and a cornice, painted pale yellow. She also used the traditional overhanging roof of terra-cotta tiles, and incorporated the vertical element of a tower with windows on all four sides that command a 360-degree view.

While the proportions and materials of this street-front facade fall within the vocabulary of the Spanish style, Martinson's expression of them is purely modernist. "I did not apply any extra ornamentation," she explains. While she left just the structural elements to express the window openings on the tower, Mizner and his contemporaries would have created rows of Roman, Venetian, or Moorish arches in their place. Where detailing was

Opposite: The house Martinson designed for the Crosses presents a Mediterranean revival–inspired facade to the street, but becomes increasingly modern in style as it wraps around to the side and back.

An overhanging roof of terra-cotta tile, a three-story tower, and tripartite division of the facade into base, piano nobile, and cornice all lend the facade a Mediterranean-revival appearance.

Opposite: A commissioned site-specific sculpture designed and constructed by Stephan Dean for the Crosses forms a transparent screen rising up the middle of the scissor stair.

needed to emphasis certain facade elements, Martinson used nondecorative molding. "I used negative detailing as opposed to positive detailing," she points out, indicating areas where the blocks above the windows are recessed, in contrast to the elaborate braided and haute-relief window surrounds favored by early-twentieth-century Spanish-style architects. While Martinson did include pilasters to define the stair tower, these are flat, suppressed vertical elements that interweave with the horizontal plane of the wall.

While the street-front facade of the house satisfied the subdivision's stylistic mandates, the remainder of the house offers something quite different from the Mediterranean revival style. "As I moved around to the eastern elevation and the south, the house transformed to a Modernist vocabulary," the architect explains. "There are planes penetrating into the house; larger expanses of glass, as opposed to isolated apertures punched into the concrete block; whole walls of glass that capitalize on the view and create a sense of interior-exterior transparency."

The rear elevation of the house, with its asymmetrical arrangements of positive and negative space, windows of varying size and shape, and rectangles of stucco painted in contrasting colors, has the rhythmic, nonobjective energy of a Piet Mondrian painting. And yet, this purely modern facade bears some spatial resemblance to those of the early-twentieth-century Mediterranean revival. Like her predecessors, Martinson creates tension between horizontal and vertical mass by balancing an upward-thrusting tower with deep eaves and a wide span of windows. Although her open-air spaces are minimalist porches roofed with cantilevered slabs, they are placed where earlier architects might have constructed loggias decorated with columns and arches.

However, Martinson's use of steel-reinforced concrete and plate glass to create a facade that suggests a dynamic interaction between interior and exterior space diverges completely from her revivalist predecessors. The architect penetrates the rear wall of the house with a thin, cantilevered slab of cement that forms a roof over the lap pool on the exterior and divides a wall of windows on the interior. With large windows wrapping around two corners of the double-story living room, the interior seems to melt with almost unfettered transparency into the green tropical surroundings.

The original owners who relocated to New York after living in the house for only a few months (when Mr. Cross, former president of the Miami Heat, became president of the New York Jets), decorated it in spare modernist style during their residence. Mies van der Rohe's black leather and chrome Barcelona chairs looked as appropriate there as they did in the great architect's Barcelona Pavilion, built in 1928–29. A collection of

A three-story scissor stair zigzags up through the tower, creating a dynamic visual element in the open-plan interior of the house.

Opposite: *The rear elevation of the Cross house is rigorously modern, with its dramatic tension of horizontal and vertical elements and positive and negative space.*

contemporary art, including an abacus-like sculpture that rises between the scissor stairs in the three-story tower, incorporates the bright colors favored by Mondrian and Gerrit Rietveld.

"We believe the house is a uniquely modern approach to a Mediterranean community [that] introduces elements of verticality and urban living into the predominantly horizontal south Florida landscape," wrote the Crosses when they recommended their home for an award for excellence from the Florida chapter of the American Institute of Architects (AIA). "All in all, . . . a dream house come true," they concluded in their letter of recommendation for Martinson, who has received four State of Florida AIA awards for her work.

Palazzo delle Aquile

*An Early-Twenty-First-Century Mediterranean Revival Mansion
in Winter Park*

THE HOME OF MICHAEL ABBOTT

Among Florida's earliest resorts, Winter Park features one of the most eclectic
architectural mélanges in the state. Founded in 1881 and incorporated six years later, the
town's relatively elevated terrain, clear lakes, and deep pine groves quickly attracted
wealthy northeastern and midwestern winter visitors. These part-time residents imported
their architectural tastes to the near virgin terrain bisected by the South Florida Railroad
in 1880. Stick-style, shingle-style, second-empire Baroque, steamboat Gothic, Eastlake,
Tudor revival, French Provincial, even Prairie-style buildings took root on irregular plots
of land clustered around picturesque lakes and meandering roadways.

But the official selection of the Spanish revival as the dominating architectural
influence upon Winter Park's Rollins College from 1930 to the present ensured that this
style would have an enduring influence upon the town. Sophisticated Iberian villas and
rustic country-Spanish-style dwellings hug the hills and overlook the lakes. While some
of the town's favored architects, including Gamble Rogers, preferred unalloyed Spanish
fantasies, others dabbled in Mediterranean mixed marriages, combining the severe
elegance of Andalusian palacios with the decorative excesses of Venetian palazzos and
Florentine villas. It is this exuberant spirit of early-twentieth-century Mediterranean
revival that imbues the home of interior designer Michael Abbott, cofounder of Winter
Park–based Marc-Michaels Interior Design, built nearly a century after the style was born.

Viewed from the street, the ochre-colored stucco mansion offers a tantalizing facade
of ogee-arched openings set in irregular planes that project and recede in a play of light
and shadow. Shallow pitched roofs covered in rosy umber barrel tiles rise to a variety of
heights, from a tall central campanile to an earth-hugging wing. A cusped arch of the type
Renaissance Venetian architects borrowed from their trade partners across the
Mediterranean divides the base of the campanile, leading to a polygonal entry court
surrounded by towering walls and projecting bays. The full language of the
Mediterranean revival speaks from the walls of this courtyard, which is embellished with
braided columns, Gothic, Roman, and Moorish arches, and a quatrefoil fountain set in a
mosaic surround.

*Opposite: Roman, Gothic,
and Moorish arches reflect
pan-Mediterranean
influences in a forecourt
guarded by a formidable
statue of a bristling boar.*

Doors of carved wood with ornamental nail heads were popular on both sides of the Mediterranean, as were twisted columns, adopted by Venetian architects from Byzantine realms.

Opposite: *Ancient and contemporary architecture meet in this foyer where a minimalist, rectangular opening framing a sinuous staircase contrasts with the Moorish arches and Gothic screens ornamenting another wall.*

The lakeside facade of the house offers a surprising contrast, with its peaceful, near-perfect symmetry and restrained paired loggia flanking a long central courtyard. The interior provides a balance of these two impulses, blending decorative dynamism with spatial sophistication. The resulting atmosphere reflects the combined influences of Coral Gables–based architect Carlos Martin; resident Michael Abbott, an antiques collector with Old World tastes; and his business partner S. Marc Thee, a modernist-leaning interior designer who collaborated on the design the house.

Borrowing from both Andalusian and Venetian palace design, Palazzo delle Aguile, named for the bald eagles that nested on the spot for several years, abounds in transitional spaces—forecourt, entrance hall, stair tower, and others. An almost narrative sense of space unfolds in the sequence of architectural events that draws the visitor into the architect and designer's sense of romance and drama. While the street-front facade beckons the visitor across a long green lawn, the forecourt creates a cloistered embrace. The unobstructed sun and moon shine down from above, while the glowing stucco walls encircle the visitor. A heavy Moorish door of studded wood opens into the cool stone entrance hall, a shadowy space from which bright rooms and a circular staircase illuminated by clerestory windows glow through varied apertures.

A spare, modernist opening frames the sinuous silhouette of the circular stair; stone ogee arches and a screen of Gothic arches offer glimpses of the spacious living room that spans from the entrance hall to the rear courtyard. This room is reminiscent of the Venetian palazzos that Abbott toured in Venice while studying Mediterranean architecture. Groin-vaulted arches outlined with braided masonry form Venetian-style fenestration overlooking an extended vista of water elements: fountains, pool, and lake. Hand-carved stone columns support the Gothic-arched windows and doorways of the room and a custom-made marble fireplace ornamented with lions' heads forms a dramatic centerpiece along one wall.

As a seaport connecting the western world with the oriental one, Venice fostered eclectic tastes among its wealthy families. This spirit of eclecticism infuses Mr. Abbott's living room, where contemporary furniture shares the travertine marble floor with a low Chinese table, a gilt Italian console table, Louis XVI chairs, and a Persian carpet. Antique

Opposite: With its coved ceiling decorated in a Pompeian color scheme and Italian Renaissance–inspired floor of red onyx, black marble, and gold granite, the dining room is the house's most purely Italianate chamber.

Above: The palatial living room, floored with cross-cut travertine marble softened with a Safavieh carpet, abounds in Venetian detail, including the groin-arched windows overlooking the courtyard's fountain.

Chinese figures, Ming porcelain, and a painting of St. Mark's Basilica in Venice continue the crosswinds theme in the room's artwork. "I buy a truly eclectic mix," says Mr. Abbott, "mostly Asian-inspired objects that express a quality of rustication."

While the warm gold and soft beige palette lends a sense of restraint to the grand living room, the adjacent dining room, entered through columned arches, gives way to unfettered Italianate splendor. The floor is decorated in an intricate geometric pattern of red onyx, black granite, and gold limestone reminiscent of Florence. Griffons and interlacing tendrils cover the panels of a coved ceiling painted in shades of celestial blue, deep gold, and blood red. A massive chandelier drops from the ceiling, its many lights reflected in the antiqued mirrors covering one end of the room.

Overleaf: A loggia equipped with a heated soaking pool that masquerades as a fountain balances stately antiquity with modern decadence.

Stone busts inset within gold-leafed niches lend a classical air to the master bedroom's contemporary décor.

Opposite: *The kitchen wing, with its polychrome exposed beams, Moroccan-inspired oven chimney, and contemporary cabinets and appliances, reflects the house's overall theme of blending antique and contemporary details.*

On the far side of this wall, a suite of rooms dedicated to the casual enjoyment of the culinary arts forms a long wing reaching toward the lake. The kitchen blends Old World and modern styles, with polychrome ceiling beams reminiscent of Spanish and Moorish interiors reaching over contemporary cabinets and stainless-steel appliances. Moorish *zellij*—a mosaic of cut enameled tiles—decorates the chimney above the large stove, adding another Andalusian effect to the room. The interior spaces of this wing terminate in an informal dining room that continues the kitchen's blend of Old and New World style.

Beyond stretches a loggia with paired columns and white canvas curtains that frame an outdoor living and dining room much enjoyed during Mr. Abbott's frequent parties. Tall cypress trees, well-trimmed boxwood hedges, and a pair of griffon-shaped stone seats accentuate the axial symmetry of the long courtyard that extends lakeward from the living room, parallel to this covered loggia. Another loggia, open to the sky, flanks the far side of the courtyard. Casual furniture and a whirlpool disguised as a fountain invite residents and guests to relax in the sun while enjoying a view of the terraced lawn that slopes down to the lake.

Opposite: The master bathroom is as sumptuously decorated as the rest of the house, with its tile and marble bathtub, stained-glass window, and Venetian chandelier.

Above: The lakeside facade of the house expresses serene symmetry with paired loggia—one roofed, one open to the sky—flanking a courtyard planted with towering cypress trees.

Three of the house's bedrooms also command this view—the large master bedroom suite on the ground floor, where a well-placed chaise longue provides an ideal vantage point. This room blends contemporary simplicity with Gothic architectural detail, including groin-vaulted transitional spaces, arched niches, and a carved stone mantel. Even the bathroom features Gothic and Moorish arches and a stained-glass window with Spanish-style bottle-bottom glass. Two guest bedrooms on the second floor occupy the wings on either side of the central courtyard, also blending antique and contemporary style.

These bedrooms are reached by one of the house's most delighted elements: the graceful spiral staircase visible from the entrance hall. This two-story stair tower is capped by a carved wood ceiling embellished with an Islamic eight-pointed star. Clerestory windows with pointed arch surrounds bring soft illumination into the center of the tower, where a potted palm raises fringed fronds to the light. Spanish bottle-bottom glass inset in the wrought-iron balustrade offers more exotic detail. Like so many features of this dwelling, the staircase unfolds like a well-told romance, promising mystery, intrigue, and an utterly satisfying conclusion.

ACKNOWLEDGMENTS

This book could not have been created without the enthusiastic aid and generous advice I received from preservationists and connoisseurs of Florida's unique architectural heritage. These people included homeowners who shared their houses with me and my readers, and who helped me network my way through many fascinating Florida neighborhoods; professional preservationists; hoteliers; historians; and many others. I am especially indebted to Ellen Kiser of Winter Park, Florida, and Charleston, South Carolina, and Christina Orr-Cahall for their support of this project. I thank my editor, Ron Broadhurst, at Rizzoli International Publications for cheering me on, and graphic designer, Eric Mueller of Element group for his constant good spirit and creative inspiration. Thank you, also, to Steven Brooke for taking such beautiful photographs of the varied expressions of *Casa Florida*. A short list of people and institutions who assisted, and to whom I express deep gratitude, includes:

Mary Bryant

The Colony Hotel, Palm Beach, Florida

The Diplomat, Hollywood, Florida

Historic Old Northeast Neighborhood Association, St. Petersburg, Florida

Ellen and Dan Kiser

John Kiser

Mary Miller, Science Librarian,
Charleston County Public Library

Christina Orr-Cahall and Richard Cahall

Arva Moore Parks

Preservation Foundation of Palm Beach

The Renaissance Vinoy Hotel,
St. Petersburg, Florida

Snell Isle Neighborhood Association, St. Petersburg, Florida

Julie Turner

Ellen Uguccioni

William Wing

~

Opposite: Crescent moons top silver-painted onion domes on the towers of Henry Plant's 1891 Tampa Bay Hotel.

Below: A narrow spiral staircase built of stone rises through three floors of Palm Beach's Cielito Lindo (1928), heightening its castle-like atmosphere.

Overleaf: Moorish domes and cusped arches add exotic variety to this asymmetrical facade, which also features the more common Spanish-style vocabulary of white stucco walls and red barrel tile roofs.

INDEX

A

Abbott, Michael, 192–203
Aguirrechu-Clark, John, 175–76, 180–81
Alcazar Hotel, 23
Art Deco, 33, 145, 148

B

Ball, Ed, 94
Barbour, Robert, 168
Barkausen, Mr. and Mrs. Henry G., 43
Bartram, John, 12
Bertoia, Harry, 180
Boca Raton Resort & Club, 20–23, 29
Borysewicz, Alfonse, 69
Breakers, the, 24
Brickel, William, 53
Bridges, Rocky, 99
Buenos Recuerdos, 42–51

C

Carlisle, J. F., 73
Carnegie, Mrs. Andrew, 53
Carrère & Hastings, 10–13, 73, 117
Carrère, John, 12–13
Carrolton School, 30, 93
Casa Feliz, 168
Casa Mia, 100–107
casitas, 62–71, 108–15
Caskill, Desirée, 100–107
Caya, Jean, 122–23
Cerwinske, Laura, 145
Chihuly, Dale, 70
Cielito Lindo, 4–5, 7, 116–25, 205
Coconut Grove, 53–54
Collins, John, 145
Collins, Robert E., 148
Coral Gables, 29–30, 38, 109, 112
cortijos, 167–68, 177
Courtney, Henry and Margarita, 144–53
Cross, Jay and Devon, 182–91
Curl, Donald, 25, 29

D

Dean, Stephan, 184–85
DeGarmo, Charles, 53
DeGarmo, Walter, 4, 11, 30, 52–55
DeGarmo Estate, 52–61
Dementieff, Piotr Alexeitch, 30
Dixie Highway, 29, 145
Don CeSar Hotel, 33–35
Don Quixote House, 108–15
Donahue, Jessie Woolworth, 116–25

Douglas, Marjory Stoneman, 112
Duke, Doris, 117

E

El Cortijo, 166–77
El Jardin, 30, 93
Elias, Bill, 131
Everglades Club, 16, 18–19, 25, 27, 43, 73, 83, 86, 118

F

Farley, Elsie Sloan, 122–23
Fatio, Maurice, 28, 43
Fisher, Carl G., 29, 145
Flagler, Henry, 10–13, 16, 23–24, 29, 145
Flamingo Hotel, 29, 145
Franchi de Alfaro, Luciano, 101–2, 107

G

Gelabert-Navia, José, 154–65
Geldzahler, Henry, 63
Gifford, Dr. John, 53
González-Alvarez House, 12

H

Hall, Kathryn and Ann, 124
Halls, D. Troy, 102
Hamlett, J. C., 33, 137
Harris, Jeannie and Charlie, 166–79
Hastings, Thomas, 12–13
Helander, Bruce and Claudia, 62–71
Herrera, Antonio de, 11
Hogarth, William, 123
Holt, Hamilton, 167

I

Irving, Washington, 16

J

Jackson, Bob, 124
Jackson, Carolyn Agresti, 124
Jacobs, Julius, 28, 126–27
Jennis, Stevan, 69

K

Karcher, Collene, 94
Kiehnel & Elliott, 30, 92–94, 137
Kiehnel, Richard, 11, 30, 33, 93–94

L

Lacroix, Christian, 107
Lewis & Valentine, 124–25
Lozano, Jose, 11

M

Maguire, Mel Rea, 154–65
Manucy, Albert, 12
Mar-a-Lago, 28, 118

Marc-Michaels Interior Design, 193
Martin, Carlos, 194
Martinson, Suzanne, 182–91
Massey-Ledo Studio, 99
McDonald & McGuire, 24
Merrick, George E., 25, 29–30, 109, 163
Miami Beach, 145
Miami-Biltmore Hotel, 25–27, 30
Mies van der Rohe, Ludwig, 186–87
Mizner, Addison, 16, 18–23, 25, 27–30, 43–44, 46, 73, 117, 183
Mizner, Lansing, 83
Molloy, Brian, 53–61
mousharabiya, 118
Muir, Helen, 53
Munroe family, 53

N

Nesbitt, Abram, 43–44
Newcomb, Rexford, 16
Nuestro Paradiso, 126–35
Nutting, Ellis Z., 126–35

O

Olszewski, Steven, 94, 99
Orr, Christina, 29
Orr, Mrs. William, 42–51

P

Pace (Lawler), Helen Rose, 137–38
Paist, Phineas, 30, 109
Palazzo delle Aquile, 192–203
Palm Beach, 24–25, 27–29, 83, 86
Palm Beach Inn, 24
Pardo, Manuel, 175
Parmelee, Dean, 155–56, 163
Peacock, Charles and Isabella, 53
Peacock, Jack, 53
Peacock Inn, 53
Perez, Luis Manuel, 100–107
Plant, Henry, 16–17, 24, 204–5
Polk, Willis, 25
Ponce de Leon, Juan, 11
Ponce de Leon Hotel, 10–16, 23–24
Pope, John Russell, 54
Post, Marjorie Merriweather, 118
Price, Matlack, 30, 38
Prisendorf, Donna and Anthony, 108–15

R

ranch house, 174–81
Reed, Joe and Robin, 136–43
Renaissance Vinoy Hotel, 30–33
Reynolds, Joshua, 74
Ritz-Carlton Cloister, 20–23, 29
Roberts, Mary Fanton, 28, 117

Roettger, John, 52–61
Rogers, Gamble, 37, 176–86, 193
Rogers, Jack, 167–69
Rollins College, 37–38, 40–41, 193
Rolyat Hotel, 30–31, 33, 93–94, 137–39
Romney Plaza Hotel, 145
Royal Ponciana Hotel, 24

S

Saarinen, Eliel, 180–81
St. Augustine, 11–12, 23–24
St. Petersburg, 30, 33
Sawyer, F. McM., 102
Schooley, Howard, 33, 36–37
Schooley, Samuel V., 93–94
Schultz & Weaver, 30, 145
Seale, William, 24
Seebohm, Caroline, 25, 86, 89
Simonson, Bryon F., 118, 123
Simonson & Holley, 123
Singer, Paris, 25, 27–29, 73
Smith, Franklin W., 16
Snell, C. Perry, 28, 33, 93–94, 136
Snell Isle, 28, 33, 36–37, 92–99, 137
Spanish mission style, 38–39
Spanish style, 13, 16
Standiford, Les, 23
Stowe, Charles, 53

T

Tampa Bay Hotel, 16–17, 24, 204–5
Tarbell, Ida M., 38, 89–90
Thee, S. Marc, 194
Tibaldeo, Alan, 175–76, 180–81

V

Versace, Gianni, 107
Vias Mizner and Parigi, 29, 84, 86
Villa Mizner, 82–91
Villa Zorayda, 16
Vinoy Park Hotel, 30–33

W

Wallace, Helen and Peter, 92–99
Weissman, Jody, 122–24
West Palm Beach: Helander casita, 62–71
Whelton, Mahnaz and John, 72–81
Winter Park, 37–38
Wood, J. A., 16–17, 24
Wyeth & King, 117
Wyeth, Marion Sims, 9, 28, 73–74, 117
Wynn, Cynthia, 99

Z

Zenatherium, 128, 130–31